Noble Heritage
Five Centuries of Portraits from the Hosokawa Family

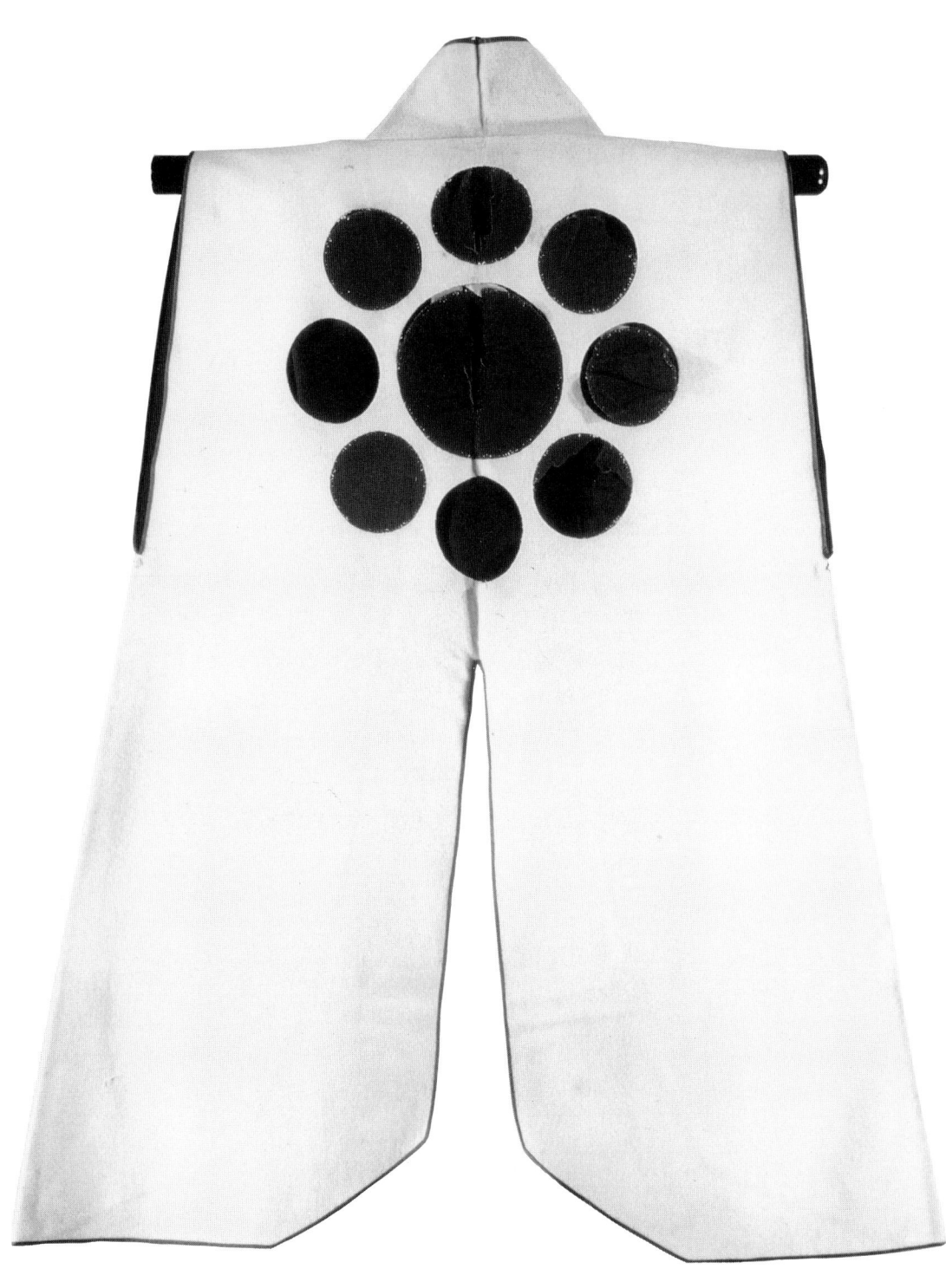

Noble Heritage

 Five Centuries of Portraits from the Hosokawa Family

Jared Lubarsky

Published by the Smithsonian Institution Press for the

National Portrait Gallery, Washington, D.C.

An exhibition at the
National Portrait Gallery,
Smithsonian Institution,
July 24 to November 29, 1992

All objects are courtesy of the Eisei-Bunko Foundation, Tokyo, Japan.

This exhibition and catalogue have been made possible through the support of The Japan Foundation, Kokusai Denshin Denwa Co., Ltd (KDD), OMRON Corporation, Japan Air Lines Co., Ltd, Nippon Cargo Airlines, Sony Corporation, Matsushita Electric Industrial Co., Ltd, Pioneer Electric Corporation, Suntory Ltd, and Seiko Instruments Inc.

© 1992 by Smithsonian Institution. All rights reserved.

Lubarsky, Jared.
    Noble heritage : five centuries of portraits from the Hosokawa family / Jared Lubarsky.
       p. cm.
    Exhibition catalog.
    Includes bibliographical references and index.
    ISBN 1-56098-209-8
    1. Portrait painting, Japanese—Kamakura-Momoyama periods, 1185–1600—Exhibitions. 2. Portrait painting, Japanese—Edo period, 1600–1868—Exhibitions. 3. Hosokawa family—Portraits—Exhibitions. I. Title
    ND1326.L8 1992
    757'.0952'074753—dc20   92-12047
                                                      CIP

Cover: Hosokawa Tsunatoshi (detail). Illustrated in color on page 80.
Frontispiece: Coat with Hosokawa crest. Illustrated in color on page 74.
Page 6: Battle flag with Hosokawa crest. Illustrated in color on page 76.

All photography has been done by Norihiro Ueno and his assistant Kohji Ohyabu, except for the one on page 30, which was done by Rolland White.

Contents

   7   Acknowledgments

   9   Introduction
            by Alan Fern

 15   Noble Heritage: Five Centuries of Portraits
           from the Hosokawa Family
           by Jared Lubarsky

 37   Catalogue of the Exhibition

108   For Further Reading

109   Index

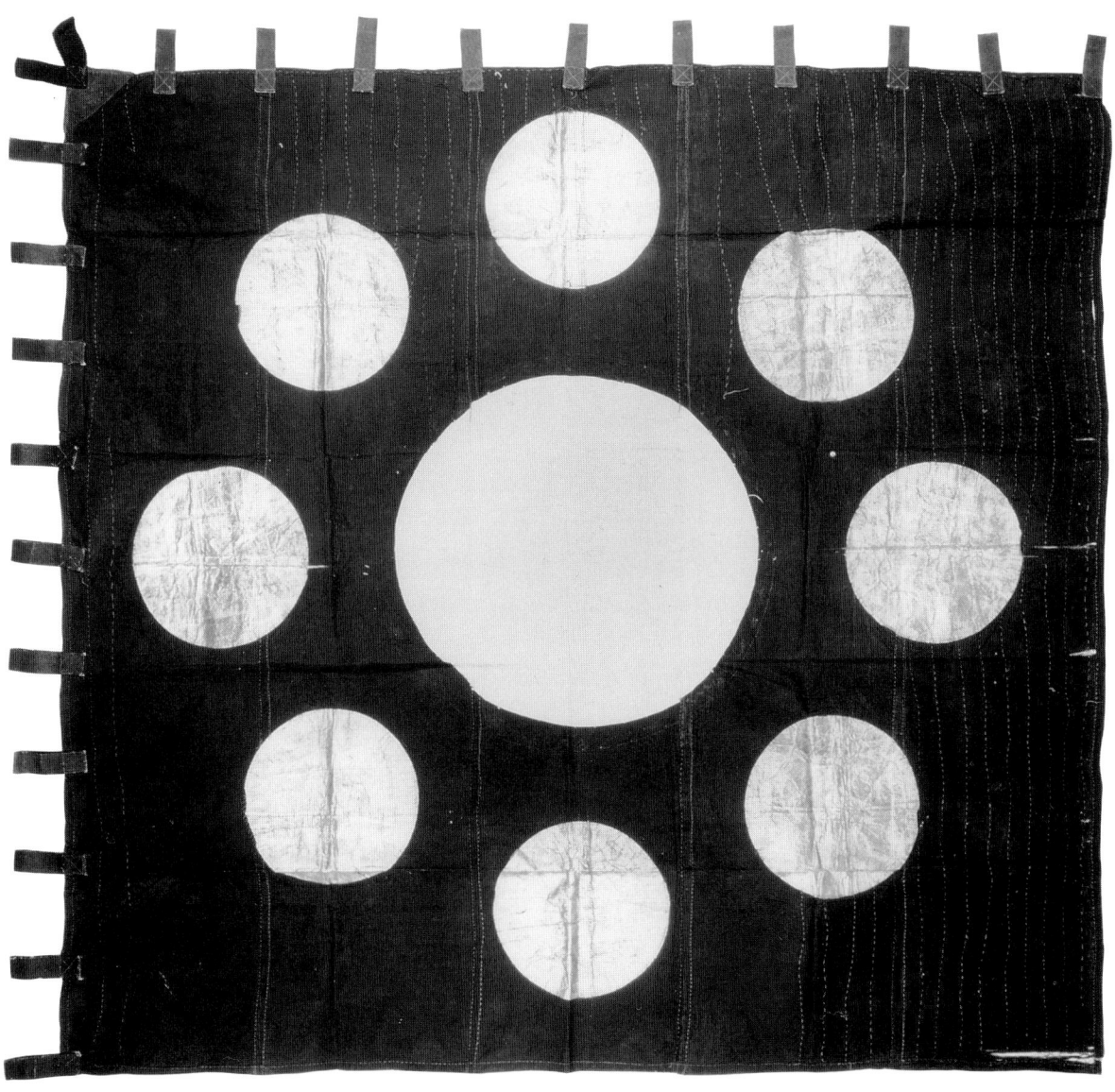

Acknowledgments

Preeminent among those to whom the National Portrait Gallery owes appreciation is Mr. Morisada Hosokawa, who first suggested the idea of an exhibition of his family portraits. Without his encouragement and generosity, we would not have been able to bring this remarkable collection to this country. We are also grateful to the trustees and staff of the Eisei-Bunko Foundation for their support of this exhibition, especially Mr. Seiichi Iizaka, Secretary General, who handled myriad essential details, from completing loan agreements to arranging photography. Mr. Akiyoshi Watanabe, Director of the Fine Arts Division of the Japanese Cultural Agency (*Bunka-cho*), was very helpful in arranging the loan of these precious portraits.

    We would like to give special thanks to the Association for Japan-U.S. Community Exchange for its help with this project since its inception, and in particular Ms. Kyoko Ito and Ms. Kimiko Hirotsu, who, with Mrs. Hanako Matano, the Smithsonian's special representative for Japan, were splendidly successful in gathering the support that made the exhibition possible. Jeffrey Stann, formerly of the Smithsonian Development Office, was also helpful in promoting the exhibition in its early stages.

    We are deeply indebted to Jared Lubarsky for his skill in recounting the complex history of the Hosokawa family, and his judgment in the selection of the objects in which this history is embodied. Dr. Warren Tsuneishi, Chief, Asian Division, Library of Congress, was most helpful in reading the text and providing wise counsel.

    We thank Nippon Cargo Airlines for subsidizing the packing and shipping costs. Mr. Masaki Shiraishi, Manager, Import and Development, Sales Department, and Mr. Toru Fukunaga, Assistant Manager, have been most helpful in this regard. We are deeply grateful to the other Japanese supporters of this exhibition: The Japan Foundation, Kokusai Denshin Denwa Co., Ltd (KDD), OMRON Corporation, Japan Air Lines Co., Ltd, Sony Corporation, Matsushita Electric Industrial Co., Ltd, Pioneer Electric Corporation, Suntory Ltd, and Seiko Instruments Inc.

    Many people on the National Portrait Gallery staff have contributed in important ways to this project: Jack Birnkammer in the Office of the Registrar; Dru Dowdy and Frances Stevenson in the Publications Office; Vandy Cook, Claire Kelly, and Beverly Cox in the Office of Exhibitions; Stephen di Girolamo, Albert Elkins, and Nello Marconi in the Office of Design and Production; and Jewell Robinson in the Education Department.

Alan Fern
Director
National Portrait Gallery

Introduction

In 1988 the National Portrait Gallery was privileged to bring a collection of portrait paintings and sculpture from its permanent collections to Tokyo and Sapporo in Japan. The response was gratifying. Thousands of people came to visit the exhibition, and considerable interest was displayed in both the accomplishments of the subjects represented and the diversity of artistic styles included in the show. During my visits to Japan in connection with this program, I became aware of the richness and distinction of Japanese portraiture, so strikingly different from American or European work, and I thought at the time that it would be fascinating to be able to complete this cultural exchange by bringing a selection of these portraits to Washington. Therefore, I responded at once when—shortly thereafter—Mr. and Mrs. Morisada Hosokawa suggested that we might be interested in showing a selection of portraits of Mr. Hosokawa's forebears in Washington.

From time to time, the National Portrait Gallery has presented exhibitions of portraiture outside the American tradition, in order to familiarize our public with some of the characteristics of this art in other nations and to suggest some of the sources that have inspired America's artists. Painters in early America worked in the style of their British or French contemporaries, and later drew inspiration from Germany and Italy. But until the late nineteenth century few painters paid attention to Asian art, and fewer still knew anything about the long traditions of portraiture in China, Japan, and the other lands across the Pacific. Thus, the present exhibition, which brings together portraits of a single noble Japanese family painted over a span of five hundred years, differs from our previous foreign shows in its disjunction from the art of portraiture in America. Instead, it presents an art in striking contrast to anything found here, and delineates a culture based on concepts and traditions all too little known in the European-based civilization of the Western hemisphere.

This exploration of Japanese portraiture, and the traditions it embodies, comes at a particularly significant time in the histories of our two nations. As the commercial and cultural boundaries of the world have shifted in the aftermath of wars, revolutions, and changing economies, the United States and Japan have found themselves—to their surprise—in fierce competition. No one would have guessed, a century ago (or even fifty years ago), that the destinies of these two countries would have become so intertwined and even interdependent. Business and manufacturing practices have been exchanged, technological developments have been shared (or challenged), and capital has moved between the two countries with unprecedented rapidity. Cultural interchanges abound. Japanese tourists flock to New York, Los Angeles, and Honolulu, while Americans roam Tokyo's Ginza and marvel at the temples in Kyoto. Baseball has become a Japanese national sport, while Americans have taken up the martial arts and have added sushi and tempura to their menus. Dr. Edward Deming has instructed Japanese managers in modern entrepreneurial techniques, Japanese capital has moved into several major American movie studios, while Seiji Ozawa, Yo Yo Ma, and Midori have become superstars in American concert halls. Yet certain aspects of Japanese life have remained unfamiliar to the American public, and perhaps this has retarded the growth of real understanding in the United States of the complex history and powerful traditions that have shaped the nation that commands so much of our attention today.

As I visited Japanese museums and collections, I came to perceive that there were several distinct approaches to portraiture in Japan. This was a natural outgrowth of Japan's earliest sophisticated sculpture and painting, closely related to the Chinese art of the time, in which the human figure played a central role. Most of these representations were Buddhas and their associated deities and guardians, but a late eighth-century sculpture of the blind religious master Ganjin, to take just one example, tells us that there were also splendidly expressive portrayals of revered individuals. Later on, paintings and sculptures of Zen Buddhist priests, poets, and holy men were presented in a highly personalized manner, depicted in all their human imperfection. And there was the formal portraiture of ruling nobility and their families, to which we will return in a moment.

A third kind of portraiture became very popular in Japan during the eighteenth century, and this is more familiar to non-Asians than the two varieties just described. As the country became more urbanized, the popular theater (Kabuki) developed a considerable following. The Noh (or court) theater was not attended by the common people, so the more raffish and available Kabuki was embraced by a considerable audience. Portraits of the most popular actors, costumed and often depicted in crucial scenes from the most popular plays, were printed as colored woodblock prints and sold widely. These portraits of the everyday, "floating" world (ukiyo-e) soon went beyond the stars of the Kabuki stage, as artists illustrated notable courtesans of the time and sneaked portraits of famous warriors into illustrations of literary works.

Any comprehensive account of Japanese portraiture would have to deal with at least these three genres—not to mention the Western-style portraiture of the past century—but such an ambitious project is beyond our scope here. Instead, given privileged access to the Hosokawa portraits in the Eisei-Bunko Foundation, we have limited our exhibition to daimyo portraiture, and to only one of the great families of that noble tradition.

In 1988 the National Gallery of Art held the first exhibition ever to be devoted to the daimyo and their culture. Mr. Hosokawa was a principal lender to this exhibition, and it was shortly after the opening that I met Mr. and Mrs. Hosokawa for the first time and began to comprehend the significance of the portraits he possessed. In Martin Collcutt's fascinating essay in the catalogue for the National Gallery show, he defined the daimyo as "feudal lords or barons who, as leaders of powerful warrior bands, controlled the provinces of Japan for much of the medieval . . . and early modern ages . . . from 1185 to 1868."[1] Collcutt points out that the word "daimyo" combines the characters for "great" (*dai*) and "name" (*myō*), and explains that the term originally referred to the absentee landholders of great estates but later came to refer to the wealthy, landed warrior leaders of various regions.

As Japanese society developed, and the system of governance became more hierarchical, the roles of Emperor, shogun, daimyo, and samurai became more clearly defined, and portraiture of these court leaders became an important activity. The Emperor emerged as the ruler of the nation and ultimately was accorded a religious as well as temporal leadership. His ability to rule devolved from the coalition of powerful local warrior-chiefs (the daimyo), who were united by a military ruler (the shogun) into a network of local estates. Under each daimyo a number of samurai served, bound by ties of family, responsibility, and loyalty. Below these nobles and knights on the social ladder were the commoners: the farmers, craftsmen, and merchants.

The leaders of the Hosokawa family first came into prominence as samurai warriors and emerged as daimyo in the fourteenth century. Still prominent in Japanese political and civil life today, the Hosokawas are one of the few families in their country to have retained their position of eminence through the succession of governmental structures that comprises the complicated history of the island empire.

After the Emperor moved the court from Kyoto to Edo (now Tokyo), the shogun and daimyo were expected to be present for extended periods of time. The daimyo thus had to leave their estates in the charge of family and loyal samurai, and maintain a residence at court. Portraits in celebration of the eminence of these warrior-nobles were required for the various residences and seats of power. Moreover, as the noblemen retired, they often became associated with Buddhist temples in the areas they governed, going there to study and to reflect; at the temples the daimyo learned the skill in written expression, in the cultivation of gardens, and in the tea ceremony that were absorbing interests of the Zen priests and monks.

Accomplishment in the arts, crafts, and writing, in addition to administrative and military skill, were virtual necessities for the Japanese nobility of daimyo rank and upwards from the thirteenth century on. Collcutt, who characterizes the Hosokawas as "among the most cultured of the daimyo,"[2] observes that the "daimyo recognized that the complete ruler's cultural superiority was as important as military or political hegemony; that it was in fact an expression of that hegemony."[3]

Since the daimyo support was important to the temples, portraits were frequently commissioned in gratitude to these noble patrons. In the case of the Hosokawas, a considerable number of the paintings now in the possession of the family's foundation came from the first and second temples in their ancestral area, from which the foundation's name, Eisei-Bunko ("First and Second Association"), was derived.

While artists gave free rein to their powers of observation in the depiction of priests, poets, and learned teachers, they were more constrained in court portraiture by the necessity to establish the position each sitter occupied in the hierarchy. Conventions of pose, setting, and costume were set and were strictly followed in most imperial and noble portraits. Nonetheless, the finest of the artists were able to communicate a vivid sense of individuality even in these court paintings.

At first glance, the American visitor to this exhibition may sense an apparent uniformity of most of these paintings in ink and watercolor on silk. While there are two or three portraits that display a different approach, most share similarities of pose, costume, and composition. The differences are subtle and will repay close study. Clearly, the artists were concerned with achieving a likeness of the sitter, and facial expressions range from contemplative calm to fierce concentration. The formal court costume worn by most of the sitters changes only gradually over the years. Several of the wives of the Hosokawas were notable in their own right, and they are portrayed in a comparably formal style. We have been able to include two portraits of Hosokawa Shigekata, the remarkable eighteenth-century daimyo leader, one in his formal attire, the other (with hand-warmer and flower arrangement) showing him in his informal clothing. In striking contrast to the series of seated portraits is the powerful scroll of Hosokawa Sumimoto, shown astride his horse in full battle armor. The latest painting in this selection, the nineteenth-century portrait of Hosokawa Yoshikuni, is derived from a photograph, though it is painted in a technique comparable to the earlier portraits; it is included here to show both the durability of the traditional style of painting and its transformation under the influence of imported technology.

Since this exhibition is intended to introduce the Hosokawas as people, not just as faces in portraits, a number of objects have been included to suggest the range of accomplishments of the subjects and to evoke the environment in which they lived. The family device, accorded by the Emperor, appears on battle flags, costumes, armor, and even the hilt of a notable sword as a mark of ownership. It is instructive to be able to see examples of armor, clothing, and objects actually used by the subjects and to extrapolate from these how the artists dealt with other objects before them. What we now think of as the most elevated traditional arts and ceremonies of Japan were adopted and perfected by the daimyo. At court, and in their own domains, they fostered the development of poetry, painting, gardening, flower-arranging, the tea ceremony, and the Noh theater, as well as the crafts of pottery and metalwork. The inclusion of a notable tea bowl and a costume tell much about the aesthetic qualities of the objects associated with these two activities in the family. And it is especially evocative to see the illustrated manuscripts of natural history research done by Hosokawa Shigekata or the lacquer sake vessel by Hosokawa Tadaoki to experience at first hand the sensitivity and creativity of these men.

In the pages that follow, Jared Lubarsky narrates the story of the Hosokawa family in the context of the history of Japan from the fourteenth century to the present. This is a complex story, not always easy to follow if one is unfamiliar with the intricacies of the political and military events of Japanese history, but rewarding in its revelation of the emergence of a family uncommonly adept in the spheres of war, politics, administration, and the life of the mind. This is a history well worth knowing as we build closer ties with our Japanese contemporaries in the 1990s, and thus this exhibition comes at an especially important time. Today, America and Japan—separated for centuries by culture, language, and national purpose—are in daily contact in myriad ways, and these portraits remind us that our neighbors across the Pacific are people deserving of our attention for their accomplishments and contributions to their nation. We are deeply grateful to Mr. and Mrs. Morisada Hosokawa, and to the trustees and staff of the Eisei-Bunko Foundation, for their wholehearted support of this remarkable venture, and to the companies and foundations whose funding has been essential to the realization of this project.

Alan Fern

---

1. Martin Collcutt, "Daimyo and Daimyo Culture," in Yoshiaki Shimizu, ed., *Japan: The Shaping of Daimyo Culture, 1185–1868* (Washington, D.C., 1988), p. 1.
2. *Ibid.*, p. 20.
3. *Ibid.*, p. 26.

NOBLE HERITAGE:
FIVE CENTURIES OF PORTRAITS
FROM THE HOSOKAWA FAMILY

Few families have played as long and important a role in Japanese history as the house of Hosokawa. Since it was founded more than six hundred years ago, this family's leaders have taken two paths to prominence: in distinguished service to the governments of their time, and in the great traditions of Japanese art and scholarship. The Hosokawas were mirrors of what Japan understood to be chivalry: warrior-poets, tea masters, trusted councillors, stout fighters—and visionary thinkers.

In the early fourteenth century, the Hosokawas were a lesser branch of the clan Ashikaga. The head of that family, Ashikaga Takauji, had settled them as his vassals in the province of Mikawa, about midway between Kamakura and Kyoto.[1] The Hosokawas could look east and west to the two poles of sovereignty in the Japan of their time. The imperial court, in Kyoto, was the center of learning and culture. Here—in theory—was the one true source of authority, the ancient ruling family that claimed its descent from the gods themselves. The military government, in Kamakura, controlled the vast estates that produced most of the country's wealth and supported most of its population. (Mikawa encompassed part of the modern-day prefecture of Aichi, dominated now by a vastly more formidable power: the Toyota Motor Company.) As a matter of form, the head of the military government—the shogun—was appointed by the court. In fact, the shogun ruled by mutual consent over a coalition of military families. His role was to portion out the rewards of faithful service, to settle issues of inheritance, and to uphold the system of feudal rights and privileges: in short, to keep the peace in a quarrelsome warrior class.

The Hōjō family, which had controlled the military government for more than a hundred years, proved unequal to that task. Within the coalition there were rivals waiting only for a suitable opportunity, a moment of imbalance, to seize power for themselves. The ablest and most dangerous among them was Ashikaga Takauji.

What gave Takauji his chance was a dynastic struggle in the court. Since the mid-thirteenth century, two lines of descent, junior and senior, had been in constant conflict over imperial succession. The Hōjō had imposed a settlement whereby the two lines would simply alternate on the throne, but in 1318 the Emperor Go-Daigo repudiated the settlement. He planned to dissolve the military government, return Japan to direct imperial rule, and keep the succession in his own (the senior) line.

After an abortive coup in 1331, the Hōjō sent Go-Daigo into exile, but his supporters kept the cause alive, reducing central Japan to a state of virtual civil war. Ashikaga Takauji was sent by the Hōjō to subdue the wayward Emperor, and it is at this point that the Hosokawas emerge from the obscurity of provincial history.

When Takauji set out for western Japan, he brought along his vassal Hosokawa Yoriharu. Yoriharu no doubt expected to play a minor part in a routine campaign, but Takauji had other plans: he had decided the time was ripe to betray the Hōjō. He seized the capital in Go-Daigo's name and with an ally named Nitta Yoshisada overthrew the Kamakura government. Ostensibly, Takauji had returned the powers of civil and military administration to the throne; in effect, however, he had taken control of the capital and proceeded to use the Emperor as a figurehead to further his own ambitions. (Until World War II, this was to be the dominant characteristic of Japanese political history: power would reside in whatever military faction could sustain the claim of acting on the Emperor's behalf.) In one stroke, Hosokawa Yoriharu left the role of provincial farmer-warrior behind him. His liege lord was now the de facto ruler of Japan.

Returned to his throne, Go-Daigo summoned Takauji to a celebration at the imperial court. The ceremonies included a kind of archery contest, called a *jarai*, and Hosokawa Yoriharu was invited to take part. The family chronicles recall that Yoriharu hit the bull's-eye with twenty flights in a row. Despite his low rank, he was called before the Emperor, where Go-Daigo presented him with his own robe as a token of merit. He was asked to shoot again and repeated his astonishing feat of accuracy. Exchanging his bow for a brush, he then composed a poem, which he offered to the Emperor.

Nothing could have been better calculated to mark Yoriharu for a special future. At court this kind of impromptu composition was more or less expected; centuries before, the nobility had relegated the warrior class to the provinces to guard its estates and had immersed itself in the better life—in silks and brocades, in moon-viewing and the intricacies of Chinese poetry, in the cultivation of an ever-finer grace and sensibility. What was there to excite its admiration in these rough-cut legionnaires from the east, who were little better than the barbarians they were appointed to keep at bay? Yet here was one who could not only shoot straight but write verse: Yoriharu had sounded the twin themes that his family would sustain for more than twenty generations to follow.

Go-Daigo's attempt at direct rule, in any case, proved hopelessly inept, especially in his treatment of the warrior class. He fell out with his patron Takauji, refusing to name him shogun, and eventually raised an army against him. Takauji defeated the imperial forces in the summer of 1336, driving Go-Daigo and his followers south into the mountains of Yoshino and installing in his place an emperor of the junior line, whose successors would then be known as the Northern Court. He then arranged for this puppet court to appoint him the head of a new military government, known as the Muromachi, for the district in Kyoto where he made his headquarters. Go-Daigo, who never renounced his claim to the throne, remained in the mountains and established the so-called Southern Court. The two opposing lines of imperial descent were not to be reconciled until 1392, when the shogunate imposed a settlement on the rival factions and the Southern Court was dissolved.

In the meantime, the Hosokawas prospered under their Ashikaga patrons, beginning with the appointment of Yoriharu as military governor of the province of Awa, on the island of Shikoku. Holding such a post under the Ashikaga shogunate called for considerable military skills. It was a reward for services rendered, but no grant of land came with it; instead, Yoriharu was given various rights to the incomes of estates in a number of different provinces. The shogun took care to send even his most trusted vassals to govern where they would be strangers, forced to assert their rights against a host of well-established local petty chieftains. Mindful that his own control over the warrior class was precarious, Takauji did not want his governors turning their provinces into permanent bases of power. Hosokawa Yoriharu was no exception.

Yoriharu acquitted himself well in Awa, governing there for almost twenty years before Takauji recalled him to the mainland to help deal with the guerrilla warfare still being waged by the Southern Court. Yoriharu died, one might say, of an overdose of bravado in 1352. Alone and without his armor, he charged a band of Go-Daigo's followers who had launched a surprise attack on the Shijo section of the city. His skill at arms could do nothing for him this time: wounded in a dozen places, he was pulled from his horse and killed.

Yoriharu left three sons, who each received the shogun's permission to establish a separate family line of his own. The governorship of Awa passed to Yoriari, the second son—whose line extends to the present head of the house. Only twenty years old at the time, Yoriari remained in the province, tightening the family grip by recruiting his own vassals among the more important local families. His elder brother, Yoriyuki (whose line is now extinct), went to Kyoto to serve the shogunal court.

Yoriyuki's talents and ambitions would raise the family to even greater prominence By imperial appointment, the shogun was nominally the military head of state, but in fact he was little more than the first among equals in a coalition of powerful lords, or daimyos.[2] Unlike the later Tokugawa dynasty (1603–1867), the Ashikaga shoguns held no vast provinces as personal fiefs; instead, they held power largely through personal and extended family relationships. Important policy decisions were made by a council of chief vassals, presided over by a deputy shogun called a *kanrei*. As the shogun's own position grew weaker, the post of *kanrei* came

Hosokawa Family Tree

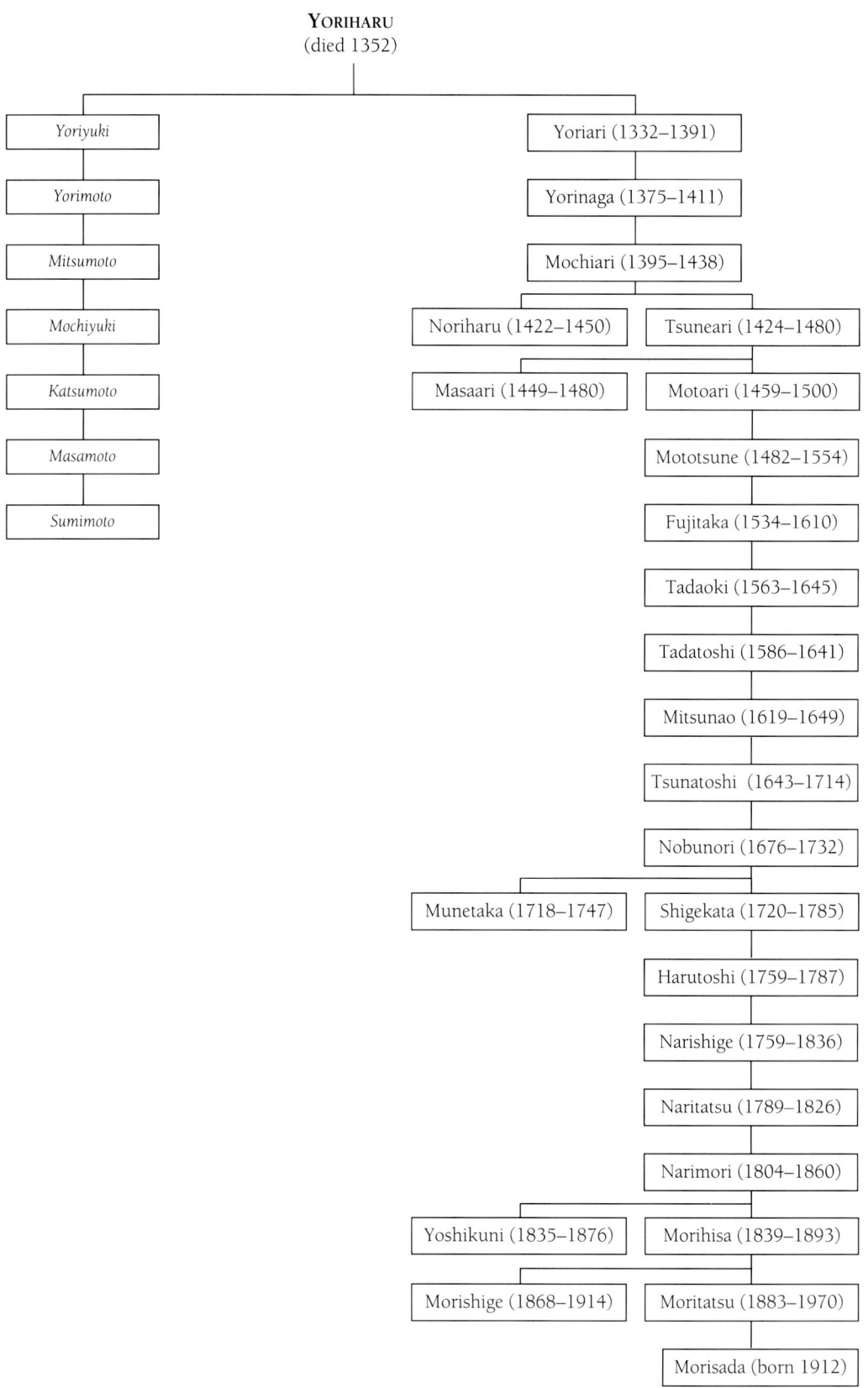

to be shared in rotation by three prominent families, members of the Ashikaga inner circle: the Shibas, the Hatakeyamas, and the Hosokawas. In time, the statecraft of Yoriyuki made the Hosokawas by far the most powerful of the three.

Ashikaga Takauji died in 1358. His heir, Yoshiakira, who would survive him by only ten years, appointed Hosokawa Yoriyuki mentor to his infant son, Yoshimitsu. Tradition has it that Yoshiakira, on his deathbed, summoned both the Hosokawa chieftain and Yoshimitsu. To the former he said, "I give you a son," and to the latter, "I give you a father."[3] No father and son could have been less alike. Yoriyuki was the very image of the faithful retainer, a warrior of the eastern provinces, and something of a Puritan. Contentious and stiff, he made enemies easily. (The powerful Buddhist clergy, for example, aligned against him when he blocked the attempts of the temples to broaden their influence in government.) Yoshimitsu was a child of the capital. Proud and self-indulgent, he preferred the society of courtiers to the companionship of soldiers. An avid collector of titles and patents of nobility, he may well have had an eye on the throne itself. He became a patron of the arts, and his villa in the Kitayama section of Kyoto, the Hana-no-Gosho (Palace of Flowers), rivaled the imperial court as the cultural center of the city.

In aping the nobility, Yoshimitsu was as shrewd as he was vainglorious. He realized that his government's only real source of strength was its association with the court. The court in turn had no real power, but it did have enormous prestige as an arbiter of taste. Those daimyos he could not bind to him by fear or feudal obligation he would bind with the seductions of culture and style. Eventually Yoshimitsu was able to compel most of his provincial governors to have full-time establishments of their own in the capital. The daimyos found their enforced habitation congenial: the provinces had made them rich and strong; Kyoto made them enthusiastic consumers of art and leisure. The age of the Ashikaga shogunate (1338–1573) saw the flowering of nearly everything that we associate with the classical culture of Japan: Noh drama, monochromatic painting, the tea ceremony, garden and landscape design, the *shōin* (villa) style of domestic architecture—all have their beginnings here. The shogunal palace was a salon as brilliant as any the world has ever seen. The inner circles of power in Japan were open to families—like the Hosokawas—that produced not only warriors, but artists and scholars as well.

Yoshimitsu and Hosokawa Yoriyuki seem to have gotten on well, despite their differences. Yoriyuki, in any case, was a remarkably capable regent. The other warrior families that constituted the support of the Ashikaga regime concerned themselves mostly with adding to their own estates, but Yoriyuki took a larger view of the welfare of the realm. He managed to settle—for a time—the conflicting claims to land in the provinces that had been a major source of dissension among the great houses. He devised reliable sources of tax revenue for the military government—which was chronically short of funds. More importantly, he turned the office of the *kanrei* into a crucial instrument of mediation, preserving the delicate balance of power between the shogun and the clans. By 1379, when Yoshimitsu was ready to rule in his own right, Yoriyuki had been *kanrei* for nearly twelve years and had put the Muromachi shogunate on as solid a base, financially and politically, as it would ever achieve.

There is far less to say about Yoriari, the younger brother who remained in Shikoku to secure the family fortunes—except that he, like his father, must have been a formidable soldier. During the wars of the Northern and Southern Courts he so distinguished himself at the Battle of Nimanzan, near Hiroshima, that the Emperor Go-Komatsu presented him with the imperial battle standard, a brocade pennant called a *mihata*. The only one of its kind to survive, the original pennant is still preserved among the Hosokawa family treasures. Yoriari also proved to be, like Yoriyuki, a faithful steward. The domains that he governed embraced roughly the northwestern half of Shikoku, along the inland sea; the region boasted rich fisheries and good land for rice and indigo. The Hosokawas had no roots here, but they would eventually learn how to prosper. Yoriari's chief concern was to subdue the numerous local families that had their own claims to the wealth of the estates. It did no harm to have a brother in virtual control of the government in Kyoto; he could count on the shogunate to leave him to his own affairs.

For as long as the post of *kanrei* served as the voice of consensus in the council of senior families, the Muromachi shogunate remained relatively strong and stable. The balance of forces began to collapse, however, with the accession in 1428 of shogun Yoshinori, who tried to take a more direct role in the policy-making process. In 1441 Yoshinori accepted an invitation to the Kyoto villa of one of his vassals, a daimyo named Akamatsu, who, disgruntled over the confiscation of some family estates, murdered him and fled the city to his own stronghold in the provinces. Yoshinori's sons, Yoshikatsu and Yoshimasa, were eight and six years old, respectively, when their father was assassinated. The shogunal deputy at this time was Hosokawa Mochiyuki, the great-grandson of Yoriyuki.

Mochiyuki held the post at an especially turbulent time. Not the least of his problems was a series of peasant uprisings. The violence was directed initially at the merchants and moneylenders who had reduced the villages of central Japan to poverty, but the revolts spread through the countryside, and eventually bands of peasants were attacking Kyoto itself. Far from protecting the city, soldiers of the shogunal guard took the opportunity instead to loot the warehouses of the rich. Mochiyuki was presiding, in short, over a center that could not hold. He died the following year, in 1442, and the office of *kanrei* passed for a time to the rival clan of Hatakeyama. Mochiyuki's successor, Hosokawa Katsumoto, was still a minor when his father died—and only sixteen when he replaced Hatakeyama Mochikuni as *kanrei* in 1445, to administer the government for the child-shogun Yoshimasa.

Over the next ten years, Mochikuni and Katsumoto were to trade the post of *kanrei* back and forth in a bizarre and bitter test of strength. Of the two, Mochikuni was clearly less interested in the fate of the government than in the power of his own family; even so, Katsumoto was hardly an exemplar of the Hosokawa faithful stewards and peacekeepers. He had the family genius for both politics and war, but in the end it was essentially for himself that he put this genius to work. Mochikuni's star fell, his ambitions thwarted at every turn. His hatred for the rival more than thirty years his junior must have been immense. The two houses took to backing opposite sides in disputes among the other daimyo families. What followed was an era of bloodshed and anarchy, in the final stages of which whole areas of Japan were essentially beyond the government's control.

All this was merely a prelude to the Ōnin War (1467–1493), which arose from a struggle between two rival claimants to the shogunate. The fifteenth-century *Chronicle of Ōnin* asserts in sublime understatement that this dispute created a "disturbance in the land." In fact, it split Japan into a patchwork of warring domains and petty fiefdoms that would not be unified again for more than a hundred years.

The early phase of the war was confined almost entirely to Kyoto. Pitched battles in the streets involved hundreds of thousands of troops and left most of the capital burned and gutted. The fighting then spread to the provinces. The shogunate itself ceased to be a viable political institution. By the end of the fifteenth century, the office of *kanrei*—in effect the house of Hosokawa—constituted the only remnant of central government.

One of the rich rewards of that position was the special access it gave the Hosokawas, in the fifteenth and early sixteenth centuries, to the port of Sakai—and thus to the culture of Ming China. Sakai, near Osaka, was the most important of the commercial cities of medieval Japan and a thriving producer of ironwork, arms, and textiles. Through Sakai, the Hosokawas became one of the sponsors of the enormously profitable China trade. The only official contact between the two countries at this time took the form of tribute missions from the shogunate to the Chinese court. The shogunal envoys, however, were permitted to bring a certain number of merchants along on the voyage, with their own goods, and in practice the tribute constituted much the smaller part of every cargo. After 1451 the Ming government restricted these embassies to one every ten years, each with a maximum of three ships. Between 1467 and 1520, the Hosokawas sponsored five such vessels, adding considerably to the family coffers and to their knowledge of things Chinese, both literary and scientific.

In the early sixteenth century, however, the branch of the Hosokawa family that had produced so many formidable *kanrei* left the center stage. Throughout most of the Muromachi period, the line that began with Yoriari had remained quietly in the wings. These Hosokawas kept well away from Kyoto and the intrigues of the shogunal court, improving their Shikoku domains and—victims of a decision of state made long after they were gone—leaving very little in the way of historical record.

From 1336 to 1392, Japan had two claimants to the imperial throne. For as long as the Emperor remained a political pawn, later generations of de facto military rulers did not worry much about which of the two was the true line of succession. The issue took on a new meaning, however, with the Meiji Restoration of 1867.

In the mid-nineteenth century, a coalition of families in the western part of Japan overthrew the Tokugawa shogunate. This revolution will be chronicled in more detail later on. The coalition asserted—as rebels have so often done in the course of Japanese history—that they were acting in the Emperor's name. One of their first acts when they had toppled the military government was to draft a constitution that confirmed the young Emperor Meiji as the rightful head of state. The episode of the Northern and Southern Courts, ancient history though it was, was no longer academic. The Meiji government decreed that the Southern Court was the true line of descent. The history of those families that had backed the wrong side—the Hosokawas among them—was ignored or even expunged. The first eight Hosokawas became in effect nonpersons, and the family line thus "ends" with Mototsune, who died in 1554. He had no children; his adopted son Fujitaka is regarded as the founder of a new line.

Fujitaka was actually the son of the Ashikaga shogun Yoshiharu. On his mother's side he is said to have descended from the Lady Murasaki Shikibu, author of the eleventh-century *Tale of Genji*—a courtly romance regarded as the earliest world masterpiece of narrative prose fiction. With Fujitaka, then, begins a history of blood relations between the Hosokawas and the Japanese nobility that continues to the present day. The influence of a childhood at court may perhaps account in some measure for Fujitaka's later distinction as a scholar and as a poet. His mother, however, was not the shogun's wife but a concubine, and for Yoshiharu to acknowledge him would have raised a problem of succession. Yoshiharu's solution was to marry off the no-longer-convenient concubine to a trusted ally named Mitsubuchi Harukazu, who thus acquired Fujitaka in the bargain. The boy was adopted by Hosokawa Mototsune at the age of five, in 1539.

Fujitaka became the head of the family in 1554, at the age of twenty, when Mototsune died. He was already a seasoned fighter, having gone to war for the first time at the age of sixteen, in the service of the shogunate at the Battle of Kagura-ga-oka in Kyoto. His military career would eventually include fifty-four campaigns during the latter part of what came to be called the Age of the Warring

States. The Ashikaga government had virtually collapsed; the great houses had exhausted themselves in bloody bickering. The way was open for the more ambitious of the minor warlords among their local vassals to seize the estates. It was time to form—and betray—new alliances, to remake the map of Japan. Fujitaka himself had no such desires. He seems to have decided early in life that the fortunes of his house would depend not on its military might but on the restoration of peace and order. If the shogunate was unequal to that role, Fujitaka would find someone who could effectively take its place. But which of the new breed of warlords would have the genius, the strength, the vision to pull the country together again?

In 1565 the shogun Yoshiteru was assassinated. A cousin was installed as his successor, passing over a younger brother named Yoshiaki, who was forced into hiding. Yoshiaki began looking for an ally who might put him in his rightful place; Fujitaka suggested Oda Nobunaga, a warlord of no particularly distinguished lineage but a bold and brilliant tactician who had made himself the master of the province of Owari. It was a shrewd choice. In 1568 Nobunaga marched into Kyoto with Yoshiaki at his side. Over the next fourteen years he fought his way—nominally on Yoshiaki's behalf—to hegemony over a third of Japan.

Events would teach Yoshiaki—too late—to select his champions more carefully. In the meantime, for his services to the shogunate Fujitaka was granted the right to wear the paulownia crest, or *mon*, of the Ashikaga family—one of thirty-two such distinctions the Hosokawa family still claims.[4] He was also awarded the fief of Nagaoka, just north of Kyoto. (The value of a domain was measured in units of productivity called *koku*; one *koku* was theoretically the amount of rice sufficient to feed one person for a year. Fujitaka's 3,000-*koku* fief was relatively modest but strategically important, and was appropriate to his standing as chief shogunal vassal.) His connection to Nobunaga served him in good stead in this new eminence. Other daimyos around the shogun began to see Fujitaka as a threat and planned to assassinate him, but Nobunaga aborted the plot. And when Fujitaka's castle was taken and looted by local rivals, it was Nobunaga who helped him recover his domains.

Nobunaga's military successes eventually kindled the jealousy of the shogun Yoshiaki. Fujitaka was quick to see how this conflict would have to end and transferred his own fealty to Nobunaga. He tried to mediate between his new and former patrons, but Yoshiaki rejected these advances and went to war. In 1573 Nobunaga brushed aside the shogunal army, occupied the capital, and took Yoshiaki prisoner. The fifteenth—and last—Ashikaga shogun was sent into exile; Fujitaka, still playing the conciliator, was able only to prevent his execution.

In 1578 Nobunaga proposed a marriage between Fujitaka's son Tadaoki and Tama, the third daughter of another vassal named Akechi Mitsuhide. Tadaoki was then only fifteen but had already made his first military exploits. At sixteen, he proved himself a gifted leader of troops and won the right to use the *mon* on Nobunaga's sword as his own. (That, too, remains among the family crests.) Fujitaka accepted from Nobunaga the fief of Tango, on the coast of the Sea of Japan, adjoining Mitsuhide's holdings in Tamba. He moved there, to Tanabe Castle, with Tadaoki and his young wife.

Fortune was smiling on the Hosokawas: their new fief was larger, they were allied by marriage to a strong and successful neighbor, and their liege lord was clearly destined to make himself master of all Japan. Then Mitsuhide very nearly brought the house down around them. In the early morning of June 21, 1582, he betrayed his oath of loyalty and launched a sudden attack on the Honnōji temple in Kyoto, where Nobunaga was staying. Nobunaga's small retinue resisted to the end; Mitsuhide's troops set fire to the temple, and Nobunaga, trapped inside, committed suicide. Young Tadaoki's father-in-law would go down in Japanese history as a kind of Macbeth, a symbol of treachery and poisonous ambition.

A messenger reached Tanabe Castle from Kyoto (a six-hour run) the following day, with the news of Nobunaga's death, and there was an immediate family conference. The danger was immense. Among Nobunaga's vassals were at least a half a dozen warlords who were powerful in their own right. It was impossible to foresee who would emerge to take his place, or what the consequences would be of throwing support to one or the other. The obvious first step was to repudiate Mitsuhide, for the Hosokawas could not be implicated in his treachery. Fujitaka, perhaps the better to maneuver behind the scenes, took the tonsure as a Buddhist monk. Tadaoki succeeded him as head of the family. Other than that, they could only wait and see what would transpire.

The key figure in the drama at this point was Toyotomi Hideyoshi, a farmer's son from the province of Owari who had risen meteorically in Nobunaga's service to the position of his chief lieutenant. Hideyoshi was at the this time fighting in western Japan; another important vassal, Tokugawa Ieyasu, was far to the east. The rest of Nobunaga's generals were similarly dispersed. Mitsuhide seemed to have chosen his moment well for seizing control of the capital. What he failed to anticipate, however, was that Hideyoshi would return quickly from the west. Leading his army on a series of forced marches, Hideyoshi fell suddenly upon Mitsuhide's forces near Kyoto, routed them, and ordered the extermination of the entire Akechi family.

Tadaoki's wife Tama had been sent away under guard to the mountains of Mitono, in the Akechi domains, and remained there for two years after her father's capture and execution. During that time a fierce struggle for power had taken place among Nobunaga's principal vassals. The Hosokawas (demonstrating again the family gift for political prophecy) had decided to throw their support to Hideyoshi.

Within a few short years, Hideyoshi had brought nearly all of Japan under his personal control. As a token of his gratitude for the Hosokawas' help, he allowed Tama to return from exile. Tadaoki built a villa for the family in Osaka and kept his wife there in strict seclusion. Tama, for her part, managed to create yet another potential problem for the Hosokawas by becoming a Christian.

The first Portuguese traders arrived in Japan in 1543, to be followed almost immediately by Jesuit and then Franciscan missionaries. (St. Francis Xavier, who spent the years from 1549 to 1551 among the Japanese, described them as "the best race yet discovered.") Tolerated by Nobunaga, Christianity made considerable advances in the late sixteenth century. By contemporary accounts, it claimed some 100,000 converts—among them a number of powerful clan leaders, especially on the island of Kyūshū. One of these was Takayama Ukon, a close friend of Tadaoki's and a fellow disciple of the tea master Sen no Rikyū. It was apparently under his influence that Tama also converted. The Jesuits gave this closely guarded daimyo's lady their particular attention. They sent her a Japanese translation of Thomas à Kempis's *Imitation of Christ,* and they may also have taught her to read and write Latin. Hideyoshi, however, who for a time continued Nobunaga's policy of toleration, came to believe that the loyalty of his Christian subjects was not to be trusted. In July of 1587 he suddenly ordered all of the missionaries expelled from Japan and their churches destroyed. Tama was baptized after this edict, taking the Christian name of Gracia, and she apparently kept her faith in this outlawed religion a secret from her husband for the next eight years.

In 1591 Hideyoshi rescinded his edict against the missionaries but renewed it again in 1597. It was still in effect when he died the following year. Hideyoshi had appointed five of his daimyos to a board of regents, to rule until his infant son Hideyori came of age. His death left a vacuum no peaceful process could fill, and the struggle for leadership among the regents soon became open warfare. On one side was the lord of the eastern provinces, Tokugawa Ieyasu; arrayed against him were the clans of Ishida and Uesugi.

The Hosokawas aligned themselves with the Tokugawas. In the summer of 1600, Tadaoki left Osaka to join Ieyasu in the field, leaving Gracia behind. Ishida Mitsunari, then in control of the city, attempted to seize her as a hostage; Tadaoki, however, had left orders that his wife was not to be taken alive. According to the *Hosokawa kaki,* a family history compiled in the eighteenth century, Gracia was beheaded by the commander of the household guard; her body was wrapped in silk, sprinkled with gunpowder, and set on fire. While the Hosokawa mansion burned to the ground, the company of the guard committed ritual suicide in an outer room.

Tadaoki would have his revenge at the Battle of Sekigahara (October 21, 1600), where Tokugawa Ieyasu finally routed the coalition arrayed against him.

Within three years Ieyasu had destroyed the last remnants of support for Hideyoshi's heir, taken and burned the Toyotomi stronghold in Osaka, and had himself appointed shogun. The country was again united under a new shogunal dynasty, and the pax Tokugawa was to last more than 250 years.

A Hosokawa tradition holds that on the night before the Battle of Sekigahara, Tadaoki's troops discovered an enemy patrol as they were preparing the evening meal. They doused the campfires and gave chase. When they returned, his soldiers were about to throw out the half-cooked rice and start over when Tadaoki stepped in and showed them how it could still be used. Few family chronicles anywhere afford a homier image than this—the leader of an army many thousands strong, on the eve of a battle that would change the course of Japanese history, squatting by the fire to salvage a ruined dinner.

Tadaoki was versed in such humble domestic chores because he had often been left in the care of one of Fujitaka's servants and lived in the poorest quarter of Kyoto while his father was off to war. Unlike the children of other daimyos, he grew up learning how to take care of himself. He could repair his own clothing and equipment, and he designed an improvement in conventional body armor that was widely adapted by the warlords of his time. Tadaoki's reputation for ingenuity became proverbial. During the early twentieth century, a popular brand of kitchen knife was called the "Lord of Higo" (after the fief the Hosokawas received from Ieyasu), because in Japanese, as in English, the verb "to be sharp" also refers to cleverness of mind.

The fief of Higo, in Kyūshū, encompassed most of what is now Kumamoto. Valued at 540,000 *koku*, it was larger and wealthier than any domain the Hosokawas had ever held, and they were destined never to hold another. (Even today, while the present head of the house resides in Tokyo, Kumamoto remains the Hosokawa family seat.) Ieyasu's gift, however, was not without its burdens. Protecting the fief of Higo was a task that would challenge the best talents of the family for generations to come.

Tadaoki retired in 1621, passing the leadership of the family to his third son, Tadatoshi. In December 1637 a peasant uprising known as the Shimabara Rebellion erupted in the neighboring province. Recurrent famine and overtaxation were the essential causes, but Shimabara had also been extensively Christianized by the Jesuits. The Tokugawa government thus believed that the conflict had been incited by the Church. (That perception played a large part in the shogunate's decision to close Japan entirely to the influences of the outside world, and the policy of national seclusion was to remain in effect for more than two hundred years.) Tadaoki, in any case, had seen the rebellion coming and suspected that it would become something entirely new to the Japanese experience—a holy war. He summoned his son and

Kumamoto Castle was built by Kiyomasa Kato, an expert in military architecture, about four hundred years ago. One of the three largest castles in Japan, Kumamoto was taken over by the Hosokawas in 1632.

grandson and instructed them to start concentrating the family forces near the center of the rebellion, at Amakusa. Unconvinced, Tadatoshi failed to take these precautions, and when the rebellion actually broke out, he was in required attendance on the shogunal court in Edo.[5]

Tadaoki's warning proved to be prophetic. As the uprising spread, peasants and masterless samurai flocked to the charismatic leader Amakusa Shiro, whom his followers called "an angel from Heaven." The banners they carried into battle were emblazoned in Portuguese with the praises of the Holy Sacrament. They had sworn to live—and die, if need be—as Christians. The holy war had begun.

Tadatoshi was ordered back to Kyūshū with instructions to assemble the necessary troops and transport ships for a punitive expedition. The shogunate fielded an army of 100,000 troops—levied from the Hosokawas and their daimyo neighbors—only to suffer defeat after defeat as the untrained rebels, entrenched in the Hara Castle on the Shimabara peninsula, mounted a heroic defense. Eventually, the weight of numbers prevailed: the castle fell on April 12, 1638, and its 37,000 defenders—men, women, and children—were massacred. The victory cannot have given Tadatoshi much comfort. Both he and his father had been forced to execute recalcitrant Christians in the Hosokawa domains, and his own mother had been, in her way, a martyr to this thorny foreign creed.

In an interesting sidelight to this story, the legendary Zen swordsman Miyamoto Musashi, author of *The Book of Five Rings*, was also among the shogunal forces, in the employ of the Ogasawara family, and was wounded during the siege. Returning to Kyoto from Kyūshū, he joined a literary circle connected with the

Tōfukuji Temple, and there he was introduced by one of the priests to Tadatoshi, who was also a member. Musashi became a family retainer and served the Hosokawas for the last five years (the best-documented part) of his life.

Tadatoshi's successor was Mitsunao. Under his leadership in the seventeenth century, the family fortunes remained fairly stable but began to decline under the next head, Tsunatoshi, and his successor Nobunori. From Nobunori the line descends to Munetaka, who, because he had no sons, adopted his younger brother, Shigekata, as his heir. (Such an arrangement was not particularly odd: a family could adopt a successor of any age, and in any degree of blood relation, if the survival of the house were at stake.) Shigekata was the great scholar of the family, its Renaissance man. An encyclopedist, natural scientist, and visionary social reformer, he took over the family at a desperately low point in its finances. The Tokugawa shogunate was still wary of daimyo houses that grew too wealthy; it wanted no rivals with the means to pose a military threat. Families that the Tokugawas felt were dangerously well off would be required to shoulder the burden of expensive public projects, such as roads or flood-control systems, to drain their treasuries, and Shigekata's predecessors had nearly beggared the clan complying with these demands by the time the leadership passed to him.

Shigekata's response to the crisis was an astonishingly modern program of management reform. Determined to fill every administrative position in the fief with the most capable person, regardless of birth or rank, he established a school in Kumamoto, called the Jishūkan, to train his civil servants, and he put an eminent Confucian scholar in charge. (Under the patronage of the Tokugawa shoguns, Confucian studies had become the ethical and judicial cornerstone of public service in Japan.) Setting an example of frugality, Shigekata abandoned the luxuries that were typical of other daimyo households: in one edict he decreed that meals would henceforth consist of *hitosara ichiwan*—"one dish and one bowl [of soup]." He forbade the members of his family to wear silk kimonos; instead he began raising silkworms in the rafters of his own castle and exporting the silk to raise revenues for the fief. To protect his paddy lands from the seasonal damage of typhoons, he embarked on an extensive program of forestation. Under Shigekata's leadership— much of it at a distance, from his compulsory residence in Edo—the fief of Higo was back on firm ground financially within two years. His reputation flowered, and he became a trusted political and economic adviser to the very government that had sought to reduce the fortunes of his house.

Shigekata's successor, Harutoshi, died in 1787 at the age of twenty-nine, without an heir. The leadership passed to Narishige, a son adopted from a nearby branch of the Hosokawa family. The new head of the house was twenty-eight and a lord in his own right of the 30,000-*koku* fief of Uto, on the Ito Peninsula not far from Kumamoto. His line had been established soon after the Hosokawas came to Kyūshū by a younger son of Tadatoshi's, but he gave up his own domains when he was adopted. Narishige lived to be seventy-seven (he died in 1836) but was only lord of Higo until 1810. He retired in his early fifties in favor of his son Naritatsu. Until the modern era, Japanese tradition regarded this as a step to be greatly admired. The ideal of the good life was to use one's power wisely and well and then relinquish it early to devote oneself to artistic and intellectual pursuits. (It was also a Japanese tradition—and still is—to step down purely as a matter of form. The cloistered emperors of the eleventh and twelfth centuries were deferred to no less in their retirement; they could influence the affairs of court as much as they wished, without the ceremonial responsibilities of office. The modern-day company president who resigns to take the blame for some corporate scandal retains his clout as an adviser to his hand-picked replacement.) Narishige's artistic pursuits, in any case, dated back well before his retirement; he was already a landscape and nature painter of considerable skill.

Naritatsu's grandson, Yoshikuni, became head of the family in 1860. It was his task to steer a course through the turbulent events of the Meiji Restoration—the overthrow of the Tokugawa government, the return of direct imperial rule for the first time in more than nine hundred years, and the opening of Japan to the outside world. The Hosokawas had always produced leaders who knew how to read the winds of change, and this time the need for that gift was greater than ever.

The early 1830s had been years of famine in Japan. There were riots and peasant revolts in many parts of the country; in 1837 a considerable part of Osaka was burned in an uprising. The unrest made it clear that the Tokugawa government was no longer capable of coping with economic distress or of keeping the peace. It appeared, moreover, that the country would not have the privilege much longer of working out its problems in isolation. From the mid-1840s onward, the Western maritime nations began to demand the resumption of trade. Foreign warships prowled the long-forbidden coasts of Japan, and the shogunate was powerless to drive them off. The crisis came on July 8, 1853, when Commodore Matthew Perry of the United States Navy steamed into the Bay of Edo, carrying President Millard Fillmore's request for the formal establishment of commercial relations between the two countries. Most of the daimyos wanted to resist. The shogunate wavered; but when Perry returned the following March, it agreed to a "treaty of peace and friendship." In 1859, the ports of Hakodate, Nagasaki, and Yokohama were opened to foreign settlement, and the Americans were soon followed by the French, the English, the Russians, and the Dutch.

Critics of the treaty—and there were many—did not all necessarily believe that Japan should continue its splendid isolation. Xenophobia was a convenient

First Landing of Americans in Japan, under Commodore M. C. Perry (detail) by Eliphalet M. Brown, Jr. (1816–1886), after Peter Bernard William Heine. Lithograph, 1855. National Portrait Gallery, Smithsonian Institution; gift of August Belmont IV

tool, a way of rallying the enemies of the shogunate. Its more thoughtful opponents were convinced that the Tokugawa government and its system of feudal baronies stood in the way of modernization—that Japan would have to emulate the West to safeguard its independence. When the shogunate agreed to the American demands, these opponents had an opportunity to involve the imperial court. The Emperor Kōmei refused to authorize the treaty, and it was signed against his wishes. A rift had opened between the court and the shogunate, which would grow increasingly wider in the decade to come.

What sealed the doom of the shogunate was rapprochement in 1868 between the domains of Chōshū and Satsuma, two clans that until then had played opposing roles in the conflict. Both were descendants of daimyos who had sided against Tokugawa Ieyasu at the Battle of Sekigahara in 1600. Allowed to keep their lands and titles, they had nevertheless been outsiders ever since, distrusted by the shogunate, shut out from positions of power and influence, nursing old resentments and passing them down from one generation to the next. The Mori family of Chōshū had taken the most radical stance against the treaty, encouraging the assassination of foreigners, prepared if need be to wage a civil war. The Shimazu family of Satsuma, more moderate at first but no less determined to topple the government, was the Hosokawas' nearest neighbor.

The Hosokawas, at this point still loyal to the shogunate, were caught in a dangerous bind. Satsuma was a much larger and stronger domain. It would have been a formidable enemy, but Hosokawa Yoshikuni taught classical poetry and tea to the head of the Shimazu family, as his predecessors had done since the days of Fujitaka. Even at this late date in the history of the military class, these accomplishments commanded great respect. The relationship that a master of one of the traditional arts had with his students was at least as strong—if not more compelling—than the strongest of political loyalties. In this case, it enabled Yoshikuni to remain on good terms with a neighbor who would soon change the course of Japanese history.

Yoshikuni's position was especially complicated because the anti-Tokugawa coalition had revived the ancient claim of acting on the Emperor's behalf. The Hosokawas, unlike most other shogunal vassals, had ties of blood to the court that dated back over three hundred years. Yoshikuni—whose wife was the daughter of the chief imperial councillor—found himself pressed into service from both sides, summoned constantly to councils in Kyoto and Edo, sent by shogun and Emperor alike to mediate between them and the dissident clans.

His goal was to prevent an open conflict that would give the foreign powers an opportunity to intervene. In the end, however, Yoshikuni was little more than a witness to events beyond his control. The Western powers did intervene, bombarding Kagoshima (the castle town of Satsuma) in 1863 and destroying the Chōshū coastal forts in the Straits of Shimonoseki in 1864. These defeats only fueled the conviction among the radicals in the anti-government coalition that Japan had to transform itself into a nation-state with a modern army and navy.

Iemochi, the last Tokugawa shogun, died in August 1868 and was succeeded by his deputy, Hitotsubashi Yoshinobu. The Emperor Kōmei died the following January, and his fourteen-year-old son was proclaimed the Emperor of Meiji. Backed by the Satsuma and Chōshū clans, the young Emperor issued a proclamation on January 3, 1868, abolishing the office of shogun and establishing the institutions of a new national government. Yoshinobu returned his powers to the throne and surrendered the shogunal fiefs. Tokugawa loyalists refused to accept this decree. A short-lived war between them and the imperial forces ended three months later when the imperial army entered Edo. The city was renamed Tokyo ("Eastern Capital") in September. By the following spring the last pockets of pro-Tokugawa resistance in northern Japan had been destroyed. The Emperor moved to Tokyo on May 10, 1869, and the new Meiji government—which conferred on Hosokawa Yoshikuni the court rank of commander of the imperial guard—began the work of dismantling the feudal domains.

Yoshikuni died in 1876 at the age of forty-one. His heirs would henceforth be citizens of the Meiji state. The age of the daimyo was over.

A modern view of the main tower of Kumamoto Castle. During the Japanese civil war in the late nineteenth century, many of the towers and turrets were burned down. They were reconstructed in the late 1950s.

If the Hosokawas of modern Japan have cut somewhat lesser figures on the great stage of national events, they have yielded nothing to their ancestors as stewards and connoisseurs. Yoshikuni's nephew Moritatsu, for example, who served in the House of Peers, was a noted collector of Zen brush paintings, calligraphy, and swords. In the early 1920s he also began to collect painting of the so-called Nihonga school, which attempted to combine traditional techniques of Japanese art with Western modes of expression. Nihonga found few admirers in those days. Moritatsu became one of the earliest and most enthusiastic patrons of such artists as Shimomura Kanzen, Hishida Shunsō, and Yokohama Taikan—now counted among the great figures of twentieth-century Japanese art. Moritatsu's acquisitions form a substantial part of what is now the collection at Eisei-Bunko—the repository of the Hosokawa family treasures from the fourteenth century to the present. Created as a cultural foundation in 1950 and first opened to the public in 1972, the Eisei-Bunko is housed in what was originally Moritatsu's office building, on the grounds of the family estate in Tokyo.

From 1929 until his death in 1970, Moritatsu was also chairman of the Kokuhō Hozonkai of the Ministry of Education—the committee charged with the classification, accession, and preservation of Japan's national treasures. His son Morisada, the present head of the family, began his own collection of oriental art in the early 1930s, when he was still a student at Kyoto Imperial University. A graceful and scholarly writer, Morisada has published ten books on subjects ranging from Chinese porcelain to the history of Ikebana; among them are also his diaries of wartime Japan.

Much like his ancestor Yoshikuni, Morisada came of age at a time when profound changes would again shake the very fabric of Japanese society. In 1937 he married the eldest daughter of Prince Konoe Fumimaro, descendant of one of Japan's oldest noble families, the Fujiwara. In June of that year, Konoe—a leader in the House of Peers and part of the inner circle of Emperor Hirohito's close companions and advisers since the two were children—became Prime Minister. A month later, his country invaded China.

By July 1940, Japan was poised on the brink of global war: its political parties were dissolved, and the Tripartite Pact linked its fortunes with those of Germany and Italy. Konoe, who had twice left the government in the intervening years, formed a new cabinet; he chose as his private secretary his twenty-eight-year-old son-in-law Hosokawa Morisada.

Morisada's diaries record Konoe's growing dismay at the impending conflict with the United States and his increasing distaste for Lieutenant General Tojo Hideki, his minister of war. Ultimately, Konoe became the central figure in the Peace Faction, a group of like-minded figures in Japan's military and civilian leadership that would try—in vain—to redirect the course of national policy. Maintaining contacts with this group was a dangerous game; Konoe, with Morisada often at his side, was shadowed regularly by the Kempei—the secret police. At this time, even those of high rank or noble blood could answer for inconvenient opinions with their lives.

In September 1941 Konoe, finally despairing of his attempt to avert the war, resigned again, and Morisada accepted a post in the Cabinet Planning Board, which directed the wartime economy. Late in 1943 he came to play a more important role, as personal attendant to Prince Takamatsu-no-miya, the Emperor's younger brother and a member of the navy general staff. Few people had direct access to the Emperor; fewer still at this point could or would approach him with realistic reports on the course of the war. Morisada was assigned to gather such reports from high-ranking army officers and Peace Faction supporters, and the Prince would relay these to the throne. Unfortunately, they were usually discounted in favor of "official" versions of events from the Ministry of War, until the disastrous losses of 1944 and 1945 could no longer be ignored.

Konoe Fumimaro returned to the government for the last time, as chief minister of state in the cabinet formed upon Japan's surrender; again he enlisted Morisada as his secretary. Konoe's only real role in this government, one for which he had volunteered, was to take a share of responsibility for the war. In December 1945 he was indicted by the International Military Tribunal for the Far East. On the eve of his arrest, he committed suicide. The death of his patron severed for Hosokawa Morisada the last ties of obligation to a role in public life he had never really wanted; he turned instead to his books and to the collection of his family treasures. In 1950 he formally assumed the directorship of the Eisei-Bunko. In the years that followed, he would serve as well as chairman of the Japan Ikebana Association and the Japan Art Crafts Association. A gentle, courtly man of eighty, he embodies the tradition of stewardship—the love and care for the high achievements of Japanese culture—that have guided his family for more than six hundred years.

Notes

1. In the standard Japanese practice, family surnames appear first, followed by personal names.

2. The term "daimyo" is not historically accurate in this context. It can serve, however, as a convenient way of referring in this essay to the heads of important families, like the Hosokawas, who controlled extensive domains as vassals of the shogun, and commanded large military forces of their own.

3. *Nihon no rekishi,* Yomiumi Newspaper Publishing Company, volume 261.

4. In Japan, the *mon* serves somewhat the same function as a coat of arms and is still dyed into kimonos worn on ceremonial occasions. Wearing the wrong *mon* at the wrong time was to cost one of the eighteenth-century Hosokawas his life.

5. The Tokugawas might be described as paranoid rulers with real enemies. Ieyasu had allowed many of the daimyos who had opposed him after the death of Hideyoshi to keep their lands; these outlying baronies were always a potential source of treason. The shogunate therefore required all of its vassals—allies and former enemies alike—to live every other year in Edo, becoming hostages at their own considerable expense. The daimyos came and went in great pomp and ceremony; they were obliged to maintain households in the capital in a splendor suitable to their ranks. In the alternate years when they were permitted to return home, they had to leave their families behind.

Catalogue of the Exhibition

HOSOKAWA YORIARI
1332–1391

Unidentified artist

Hanging scroll
Ink and color on silk, 1391

The first in the family line that descends to the present head of the house of Hosokawa, Yoriari left little behind to illuminate the personality behind his formal portrait. His goals were direct and uncomplicated: to govern the estates that the Ashikaga shogunate had entrusted to him; to subdue the lesser provincial families that contested his right to rule; and to furnish the needs of his illustrious elder brother, Yoriyuki, in the far-off (and expensive) imperial capital. Yoriari had good reason to be content in his brother's shadow: Yoriyuki moved in the inner circles of power, but it was Yoriari—the second son, and by an "unofficial" wife—who had the land. No matter that Yoriari had to spend twenty years at war to pacify his fief, that the income he took from it had to support not only his family but Yoriyuki's: the land—that scarcest of all resources, the measure of all value in a warrior society—was worth the price.

The inscription on this portrait dates it to 1391, the year of Yoriari's death.

 THE IMPERIAL STANDARD

The brocade pennant called a *mihata* was displayed to announce the Emperor's presence in a ceremonial procession or on the field of battle. The pennant here is an Edo-period (1600–1868) copy of the one Hosokawa Yoriari received from the Emperor Go-Komatsu in 1391, during the wars of the Southern and Northern Courts. Yoriari's victory in an otherwise minor campaign had earned him this special mark of imperial gratitude. (The original *mihata* is the oldest surviving example and too fragile to exhibit.)

Inscribed on the silk in gold leaf are the names of two Shinto deities: Tenshō Go-daijin, on the right, is the ancestral goddess of the imperial line; Hachiman Dai-bosatsu, on the left, is a god associated with military skill and prowess, who came to be worshiped at the same time as a Buddhist saint. This mixture of pieties posed no particular contradiction to the Japanese of the time—nor, indeed, to the Japanese of today. Since the introduction of Buddhism to Japan in the sixth century, the two religions have for the most part enjoyed a remarkably flexible and mutually hospitable relationship. Elements of one practice and belief are often grafted onto the other. It is by no means unusual in present-day Japan to find Shinto shrines on the grounds of Buddhist temples.

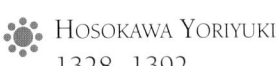

HOSOKAWA YORIYUKI
1328–1392

Unidentified artist

Hanging scroll
Ink and color on silk;
inscription dated to 1392

It reveals a great deal about this stern warrior-statesman, Yoriyuki, that he chose to have himself portrayed with a Muse. The figure behind him, holding a fan, is a *tenshi*, or angelic spirit, who appeared to him in a dream and inspired one of his poems.

Among the Hosokawas, however, Yoriyuki is not especially remembered for his poetry; serving the flamboyant young Ashikaga Yoshimitsu as deputy shogun, he may not have had the leisure for aesthetic pursuits. Even so, when he resigned in 1389 and went to Shikoku to live with his brother, it was typical of him to account for that decision in verse. The capital was a place of courtiers and drones, and he had made too many enemies there. The time had come to look inward and find peace.

Jinsei go-jū	Having passed the age of fifty,
Kō naki wo hazu	I've accomplished nothing.
Kaboku haru sugite	My spring has passed
Natsu sude ni nakabanai	And midsummer is upon me.
Manshitsu no sōyō	The room is full of bluebottle flies
Haraedomo tsukushi gatashi	That won't be driven off.
Sarite zento wo tazune	It's time I left, sought a Zen temple,
Seifu ni fusu	Caught a fresh breeze.

Alas, Yoriyuki was not destined to enjoy the breeze for long; within a year, shogun Yoshimitsu had asked him to resume his post. Yoriyuki agreed; he returned to Kyoto, where he died in office in 1392.

Noh Robe:
Atsuita Karaori

Noh went through its richest period of development from the latter half of the fourteenth century to the early part of the fifteenth, when it evolved from a type of drama centered primarily on shrines and temples. Originally it was a form of prayer for good harvests or long life, or protection from the influence of evil spirits. As an emerging theatrical art, it was taken up with great enthusiasm by the Ashikaga shogun Yoshimitsu. Under his lavish patronage the styles and techniques of Noh were codified, its aesthetic principles were formulated, and most of the texts that still constitute the main body of the Noh repertoire were written. The appreciation—and the performance—of Noh became a measure of refinement in the warrior class. In important families like the Hosokawas, Noh robes and masks were treasures to be passed down from one generation to the next.

Rules and symbolic conventions govern every aspect of Noh, including its costumes. Robes in lush colors and elaborate patterns, for example, are reserved primarily for the main character, called the *shite*. The robe here, one of more than three hundred in the Hosokawa collection, would be worn as an inner coat by an actor playing a male part, or as an outer coat for the role of a woman of humble caste. The term *karaori* identifies it as a garment of stiff brocaded silk; *atsuita* usually refers to robes woven with strong color contrasts and geometric designs.

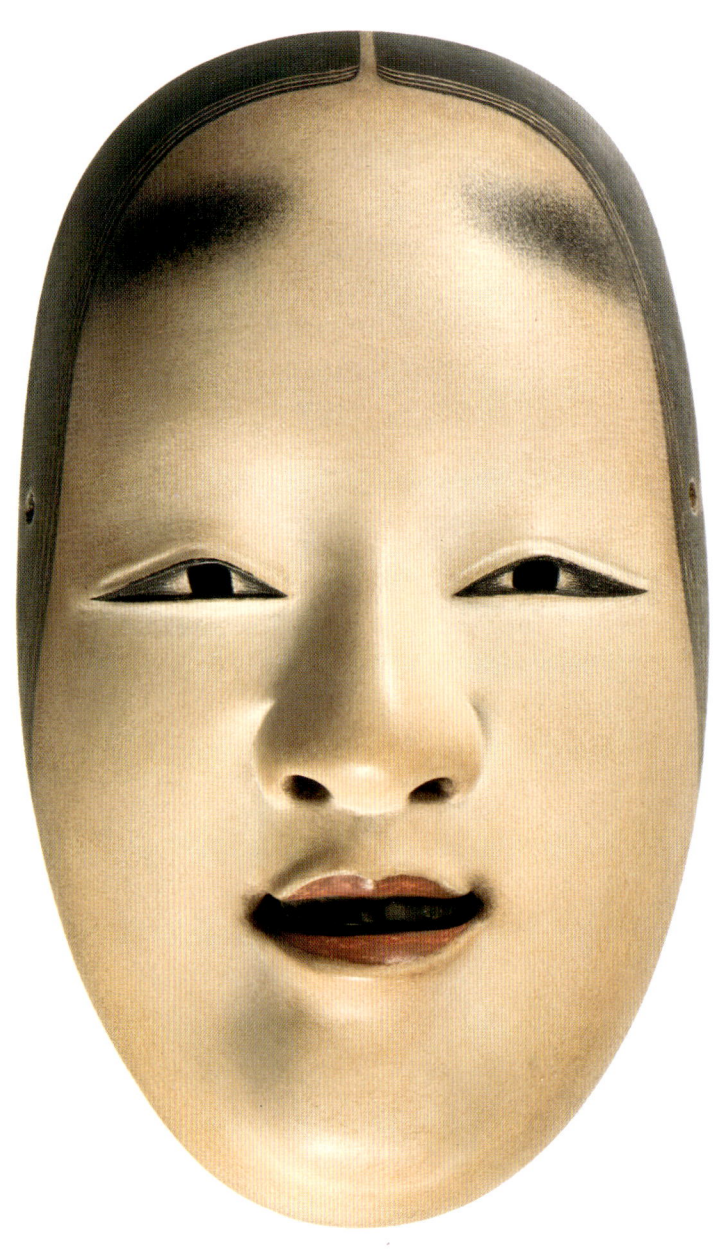

NOH MASK:
KO-OMOTE

The characters of Noh drama, if that term can legitimately be applied, are emblematic figures—the ghost of a fallen warrior, the vengeful demon, the old fisherman, the court lady—and each of these has its own mask. This one, made of polychromed wood sometime in the eighteenth century, is called a *ko-omote* and is specific to the role of a young woman. Like all Noh masks, it is made of cypress, a material chosen for its lightness and strength. The *ko-omote,* especially, is carved much smaller than the actual size of the human face: in part this is done to underscore the sense of the supernatural, the feeling of unearthly grace that the role is meant to evoke.

It was not unusual for devotees of Noh, such as Hosokawa Yoriyuki, to take masks and robes with them on military campaigns. To perform one of the plays before going into battle was an auspicious act, a way of gathering and focusing one's energies—and paradoxically, because the object of Noh was to transcend the everyday world of change and strife—a kind of prayer for peace.

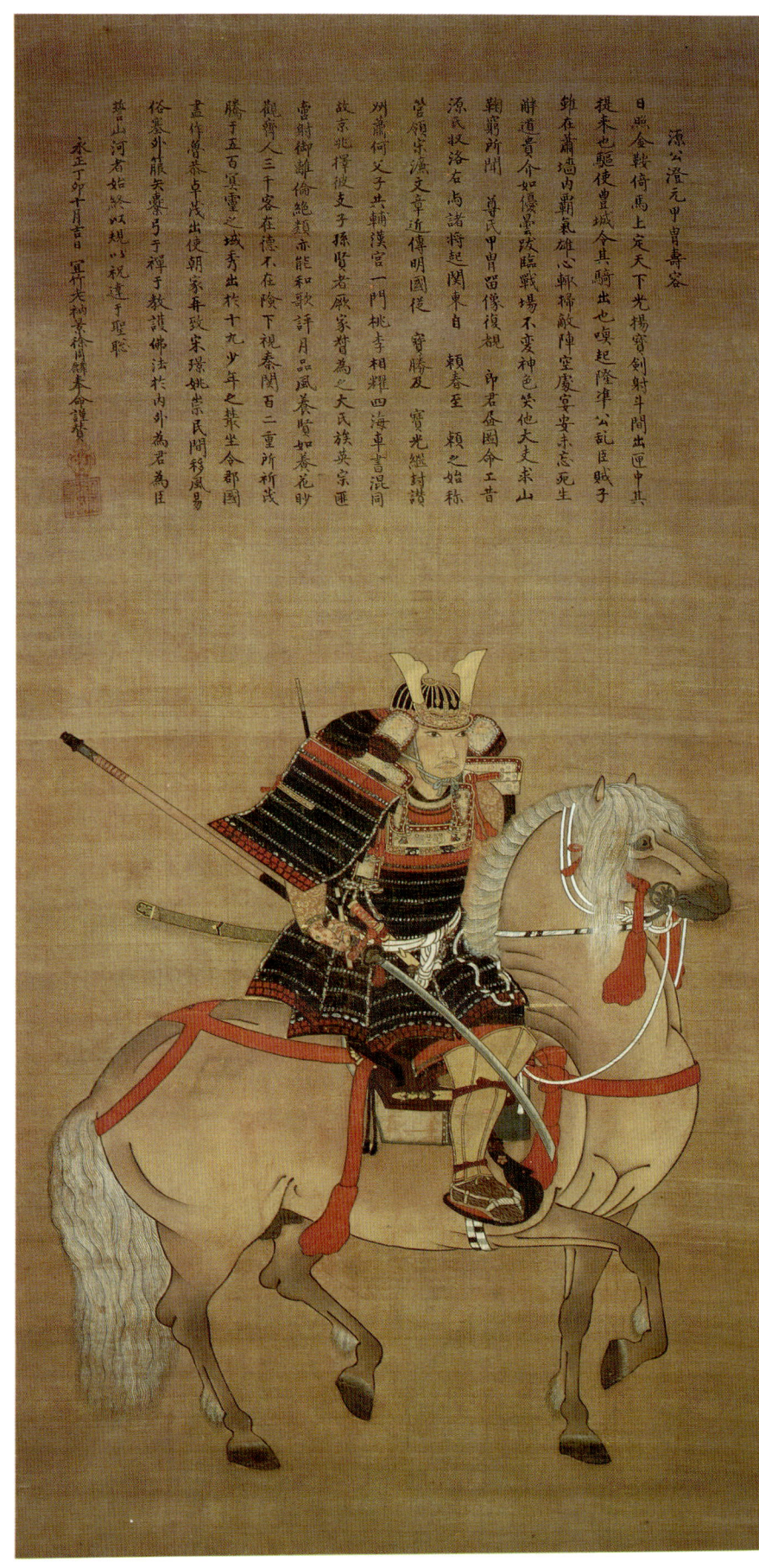

HOSOKAWA SUMIMOTO
1489–1520

Unidentified artist

Hanging scroll
Ink and color on silk;
inscription by Keijo Shurin,
Muromachi period,
no later than 1507

Born into a collateral branch of the family, Sumimoto was adopted into the line of Hosokawa shogunal deputies that descended from Yoriyuki. No period in Japanese history was as bloody and chaotic as the one in which Sumimoto lived: the institutions of central government had all but collapsed, and every man's hand was raised against his neighbor, his lord, and even his relatives. Sumimoto's stepfather, Masamoto, was assassinated by one of his vassals; one of his two brothers was killed by the other. Sumimoto himself became head of this branch of the family in 1507, only to be deposed by his surviving brother the following year.

This work depicts Sumimoto in full armor, wearing both long and short swords and carrying a halberd. It was commissioned while he was still in power and inspired by a similar portrait of Ashikaga Takauji, founder of the Muromachi shogunate and the Hosokawa family's original patron. The inscription notes that Sumimoto was not only a great archer and horseman, but a poet and lover of nature as well. Equestrian portraits are relatively rare in the Japanese tradition; this one has been designated by the Japanese government as an "important cultural property."

HOSOKAWA FUJITAKA
1534–1610

Tashiro Tōho

Hanging scroll
Ink and color on silk,
Keichou 17 (1612)

A key figure in the alliances that reunified Japan at the end of the sixteenth century, Fujitaka (also called by his Buddhist name, Yūsai) is better known today as a poet and a scholar of the *Kokinshū*. An anthology of classical poetry compiled in the early tenth century, the *Kokinshū* is a notoriously difficult work, filled with references to Chinese poetry and readable on many different levels of meaning. The loftiest interpretations of the text are passed down in secret, from teacher to chosen disciple. Fujitaka was one of a small handful of the scholars of his time to reach this level.

In July of 1600, Fujitaka was at Tanabe Castle, seat of the family domains, when it was attacked by a rival clan. The castle was held only by women and children; Fujitaka himself, then in retirement, was sixty-six. Fearing that the commentaries and manuscripts he had collected in his study of the *Kokinshū* would be lost if the castle were overrun, he arranged to give them to the imperial court. A delegation was allowed to pass through the siege to receive them, whereupon Fujitaka composed the following:

Inishie mo	In the world that remains,
Ima mo kawaranu	Past and present
Yo no naka ni	Unchanged,
Kokoro no tane wo	I leave these words:
Nokosu koto no ha	Seeds of my spirit.

Fujitaka lived another ten years. Much of his own poetry survives, collected in an anthology called the *Shūmyōshū*.

SUIT OF ARMOR WITH CRIMSON BRAID, WORN BY FUJITAKA

By the fifteenth century, the Japanese foot soldier was wearing a simple form of armor called a *haramaki,* which opened down the back. The mounted warlord was protected by a far more elaborate style, introduced centuries earlier from the Asian mainland, made of horizontal strips of iron linked together with braided cords and strengthened by layers of lacquer. This afforded him both protection and flexibility of movement, but the wide skirts made it extremely heavy. Like his counterpart in medieval Europe, he could fight only on horseback.

  Military tactics changed, and the Japanese knight was called upon more and more to fight on foot. By the late Muromachi period a new style had emerged, adopting the lighter *haramaki* of the common soldier but keeping the helmet and shoulder guards of the previous age. Fujitaka's armor here is an especially fine example. It was made by the Myōchin, a family of armorers that claimed to trace its origins back to the first century A.D.; by Tadaoki's time they virtually dominated the craft. Even an indifferent warrior, it was said, would fight like a demon at the prospect of taking a suit of Myōchin armor from a fallen enemy.

HOSOKAWA JAKŌ
1542–1616

Unidentified artist

Hanging scroll
Ink and color on silk;
inscription dated Genna 4
(1618)

Fujitaka's wife, Jakō, was a fitting consort for this cultivated warrior. Reputed to be something of a scholar and poet in her own right, she was also skilled with the *naginata*, a kind of halberd with a broad, curved blade, favored by the women of the samurai class. She was the daughter of Numata Mitsukane, head of a prominent daimyo family from the area near Lake Biwa. (Like the Hosokawas, the Numatas were longtime trusted vassals of the Ashikaga shoguns.) When the family was under attack at Tanabe Castle, Jakō is said to have climbed to the topmost level of the fortress and sketched the numbers and dispositions of the enemy forces with her lip rouge. Her portrait is unusual among those of the women in the Hosokawa collection in that it was probably done while she was still alive. While reflecting the fact that she was deeply devout, the portrait is conventional. The inscription recites her virtues and pieties; it was added in 1618—well after her death at the age of seventy-four—by a priest of the Nanzenji Temple in Kyoto.

Hosokawa Tadaoki
1563–1645

Unidentified artist

Hanging scroll
Ink and color on silk,
Kanbun 10 (1670)

Even for a Hosokawa, Tadaoki (also known by his Buddhist name, Sansai) was a figure of considerable artistic accomplishments: he was a poet, a painter, and one of the seven chief disciples of Sen no Rikyū—the man responsible for making the tea ceremony the ritual of grace and spiritual simplicity that it has become today. By the sixteenth century, tea had become the "performance art" of the warrior class: no great lord could call himself truly accomplished if he were not a connoisseur. Collectors spent fortunes, even by the standards of the day, for the bowls and accessories that the ceremony demanded.

Rikyū himself, however, who came to wield enormous social and political influence, was the central figure in one of the strangest episodes in medieval Japanese history. In 1591, the warlord Hideyoshi, who for many years had been his patron, inexplicably ordered the tea master to commit suicide. It was Tadaoki who made the necessary preparations—even to providing one of his own retainers to give the *kaishaku*, the coup de grace. Just before his death, Rikyū took from the folds of his kimono a bamboo teaspoon that he had made himself, entrusting the swordsman to give it to Tadaoki as a memento. The spoon, unfortunately, was later destroyed in a fire, but Tadaoki's collection of tea bowls and utensils, a number of them associated with Rikyū, was rivaled by few of the great lords of his day.

BLACK RAKU WARE TEA BOWL: "THE LADY OTSU"

Tadaoki laid the foundations for the Hosokawa family's extensive collection of tea utensils and related objects. He commissioned this bowl from Chōjirō I, the founder of *raku*—a style of earthenware pottery modeled by hand with thick strands of clay, rather than thrown on the wheel, and fired at low temperatures. Most examples of *raku* ware have thick lead glazes, ranging from lustrous black to red-brown. Devotees of tea admire them especially for their rough textures, uneven surfaces, and broken colors.

This bowl was given its name, "The Lady Otsu," by the tea master Sen Sotan. In later periods the practice of naming tea vessels became widespread, but in the sixteenth century it was still confined to pieces of exceptional quality and character. In one place, the lip of the bowl has been chipped and mended, but its impression of serenity and strength remains unimpaired.

Very little is known about the life of Chōjirō I. He was apparently born in Kyoto in 1516, the son of a Korean immigrant potter. The first authenticated example of his work is a roof ornament dated 1574, and he seems to have begun his career as a tilemaker. Under the patronage of Sen no Rikyū, he later built a kiln in the Jūraku section of the city, where he made tea vessels for the tea master and his fellow connoisseurs—including the warlords Oda Nobunaga and Toyotomi Hideyoshi. This work became known as Jūraku ware, and finally *raku* ware. Chōjirō lived to about the age of seventy-five; his descendants still follow the tradition he established.

 LACQUER SAKE VESSEL

It is unusual to find the head of an important family, like Hosokawa Tadaoki, turning his hand to lacquerware. While a daimyo was expected to devote himself to some cultural pursuit, he normally left the craftsmanship to others. He might admire a tea bowl, but it was beneath his station to master the potter's wheel. Few crafts, moreover, are as painstaking and difficult as lacquerware. Properly curing and shaping the base, as well as applying, polishing, and reapplying the layers of resin, are skills that take years to learn. Tadaoki's gifts as an artist, however, were more than matched by an affinity for the hands-on, practical business of life. He could create an exquisite work like this flask; he could also teach stonecutters how to shape the blocks for the facing of a castle moat.

    The flask is in the shape of an eggplant: a *nasu* in Japanese. The design is a play on words; written in different characters, *nasu* can also mean "to succeed" or "to achieve one's purposes." An old Japanese folk belief holds it an especially good omen to see an eggplant in the first dream of the New Year.

 LACQUER SAKE CUP WITH HIDDEN CROSS

The small sake cup here was made for Hosokawa Gracia, Tadaoki's wife, whose conversion to Christianity endangered not only her own life but the fortunes of her family. Gracia did not survive to see the systematic persecutions of the early seventeenth century (there was even a government Office of Inquisition, created in 1640 and charged with the discovery and extermination of converts), but the Japanese who clung stubbornly to their faith during this period were ingenious at concealing the signs and tokens of their religion. One well-known example is the *Maria Kannon*—a statue of the Buddhist goddess of mercy that reveals itself on closer examination to be a Virgin and Child. Another is this cup. Toward the lip of the vessel, the family crest (*kuyō-no-mon*) has been worked into the design in gold. The crest would normally be composed of a circle surrounded by eight smaller circles. Here, however, the addition of four small points elongates the figure, which thus becomes a hidden cross.

LACQUER DISHES AND BOWLS WITH FLORAL DESIGN

This lacquerware service was part of Hosokawa Gracia's dowry. She gave it as a wedding present when her attendant married a daimyo named Hirata, from what is now Tottori Prefecture. Very few written records of Gracia exist. In 1979 Hosokawa Morisada, the present head of the family, contacted the Hirata descendants to ask if any of her letters to this attendant had survived. There was, he was told, a small paulownia-wood chest. When the chest was brought to the Eisei-Bunko, the family repository in Tokyo, and opened, these pieces were found inside. The small dishes were used for sweets, to serve with tea. Of the two covered bowls, the larger would normally be for rice and the smaller for soup. The floral design of the set is done in colored lacquer. The pattern of circles on the bowls would have to have been added after Gracia married Tadaoki, since it was he who adopted the design as the family crest.

SUIT OF ARMOR
INSPIRED BY TADAOKI

The redoubtable Tadaoki's devotion to the arts should not obscure his career as a soldier. Between 1578 and 1600 he took part in more than fifty campaigns. It was a period of radical change in the nature of warfare, prompted by the discovery that musket fire by massed ranks of infantry could be used to devastating effect. Tadaoki's observation of battle wounds inspired this suit of armor—so successful an improvement on existing styles (the suit owned by his father, Fujitaka, is a good example) that it was soon widely copied. His innovation lay in the design of the sections protecting the arms and legs. They were made of rounded lengths of iron, banded with strips of leather, that would either deflect a musket ball or, if it penetrated, result in a less traumatic wound. We can sense in this "modern armor," as it was called at the time, the kind of campaigner Tadaoki must have been. There are no ornamental shoulder pieces; it is simple, sturdy, and utilitarian. Nor was Tadaoki the kind of commander to lead from the rear. The right arm of the suit has been repaired, where it received the thrust of a lance in the Battle of Sekigahara in 1600.

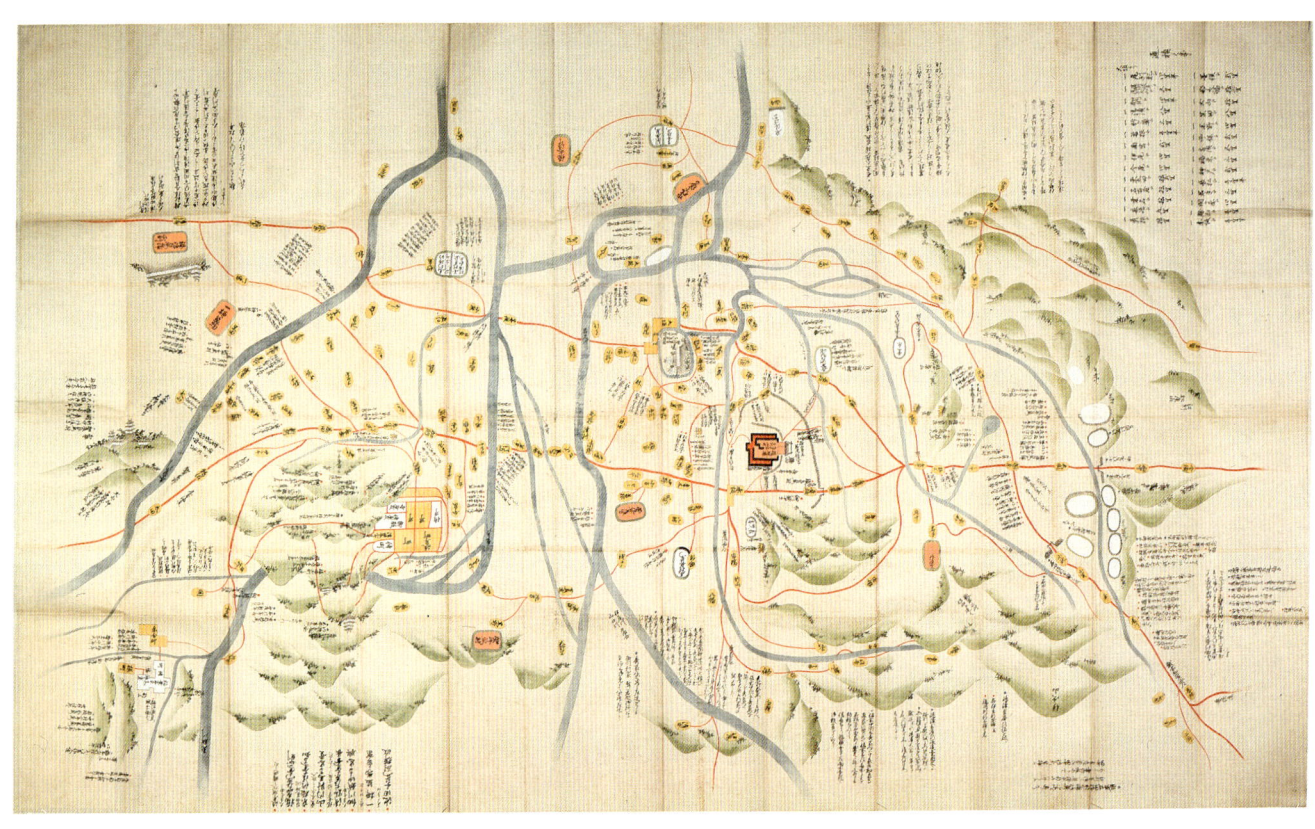

THE BATTLE OF
SEKIGAHARA

After the death of the warlord Toyotomi Hideyoshi, there was a falling-out among the five men appointed to act as regents for his infant son. On one side were the Ishida, Uesugi, and Shimazu clans and their allies in western Japan; on the other was Tokugawa Ieyasu, lord of the Kantō—the huge estates of the eastern plain. The decisive battle between them took place on October 21, 1600, at Sekigahara, in the mountains of present-day Gifu Prefecture, between Nagoya and Kyoto. The result was a crushing victory for Ieyasu and his generals—one of whom was Hosokawa Tadaoki. The map shown here, made soon after the battle, traces in detail the movement of the armies that began on the day before. Ieyasu's main strength is indicated by the red mark in the middle. On the morning of the October 21, Tadaoki took part in the advance on Ieyasu's right flank, attacking from a mountainous position that commanded a key road called the Kitaguni Kaidō. In the heat of the ensuing battle, the daimyo leaders of five opposing armies switched sides, and the attack became a rout.

In the lower right-hand corner of the map is a poem that Ieyasu composed on his victory:

Teki ni katte   His enemies defeated,
Yama ni habikoru   Spread over the mountains
 Matsudaira   like a field of pines,
Chiyo yorozu yo wo   Ieyasu will live on
Tsuzuke Ieyasu   For a thousand years—nay
                          to the end of time.

Ieyasu died sixteen years later. The dynasty he had founded collapsed in 1867.

HOSOKAWA TADATOSHI
1586–1641

Unidentified artist

Hanging scroll
Ink and color on silk;
inscription dated to 1644

In 1600, as a reward for the family support, the first Tokugawa shogun Ieyasu had given Hosokawa Tadaoki the rich fief of Buzen, on the island of Kyūshū. In 1632, when the leadership of the family had passed to his son Tadatoshi, that gift was exchanged for another, even richer: the Hosokawas were granted the domains of Higo, in present-day Kumamoto Prefecture—a move that nearly doubled their fortunes. Once again, however, they were strangers in the land, and the fief of Higo was notoriously hard on strangers. There was a lesser local gentry here, well entrenched and jealous of its prerogatives. One way or another, every previous outsider imposed upon it had come to grief. (The Kato family, which the Hosokawas replaced, was dissolved for plotting against the Tokugawa government.) Tadatoshi, however, proved to be a leader with consummate diplomatic skills. His treatment of the local gentry won him their loyalty and respect. His genius for political administration earned him a place as adviser to the shogunate, and he became a close personal confidant of the third Tokugawa shogun Iemitsu. His descendants went on to rule the fief of Higo untroubled for more than two hundred years, until the collapse of the feudal system itself.

 Kamishimo Owned by Tadatoshi

Under the Tokugawa shoguns, the *kamishimo*—literally "upper and lower garment"—became the official garb of the warrior class, to be worn over a kimono on formal and ceremonial occasions. It was normally made of hemp, stencil-dyed in small, intricate geometric patterns. Often a particular pattern would be exclusive to one daimyo family and its retainers. The upper part of the *kamishimo* is a kind of sleeveless cape; the wide, winglike shoulders are stiffened with whalebone. The owner's family crest appears in the center of the back and on both shoulders. The two long, narrow front panels are belted tightly into the pleated trousers, called *hakama*; the trousers, cut like culottes, are considerably longer than the wearer's legs, thus hampering his movements. Some scholars see this as a deliberate device to curb the warrior's normally quarrelsome temper. Be that as it may, in formal *hakama* one could hardly be otherwise than sedate.

COAT WITH HOSOKAWA CREST OWNED BY TADATOSHI

Surcoats of this type, called *jimbaori,* were worn by warlords of the fifteenth and sixteenth centuries over their armor, when they wished to cut even more imposing figures on bivouac in the field. It was a period much like the present, when things European made a strong appeal to the Japanese sense of high style. Dutch and Portuguese traders had established a foothold in western Japan, and the warlords often had these surcoats made of imported fabric, such as wool or velvet. Occasionally the coats sported high collars or buttons—or even epaulets. Tadatoshi's surcoat is white twill, appliquéd with black circles to form the *kuyō-no-mon,* the family crest.

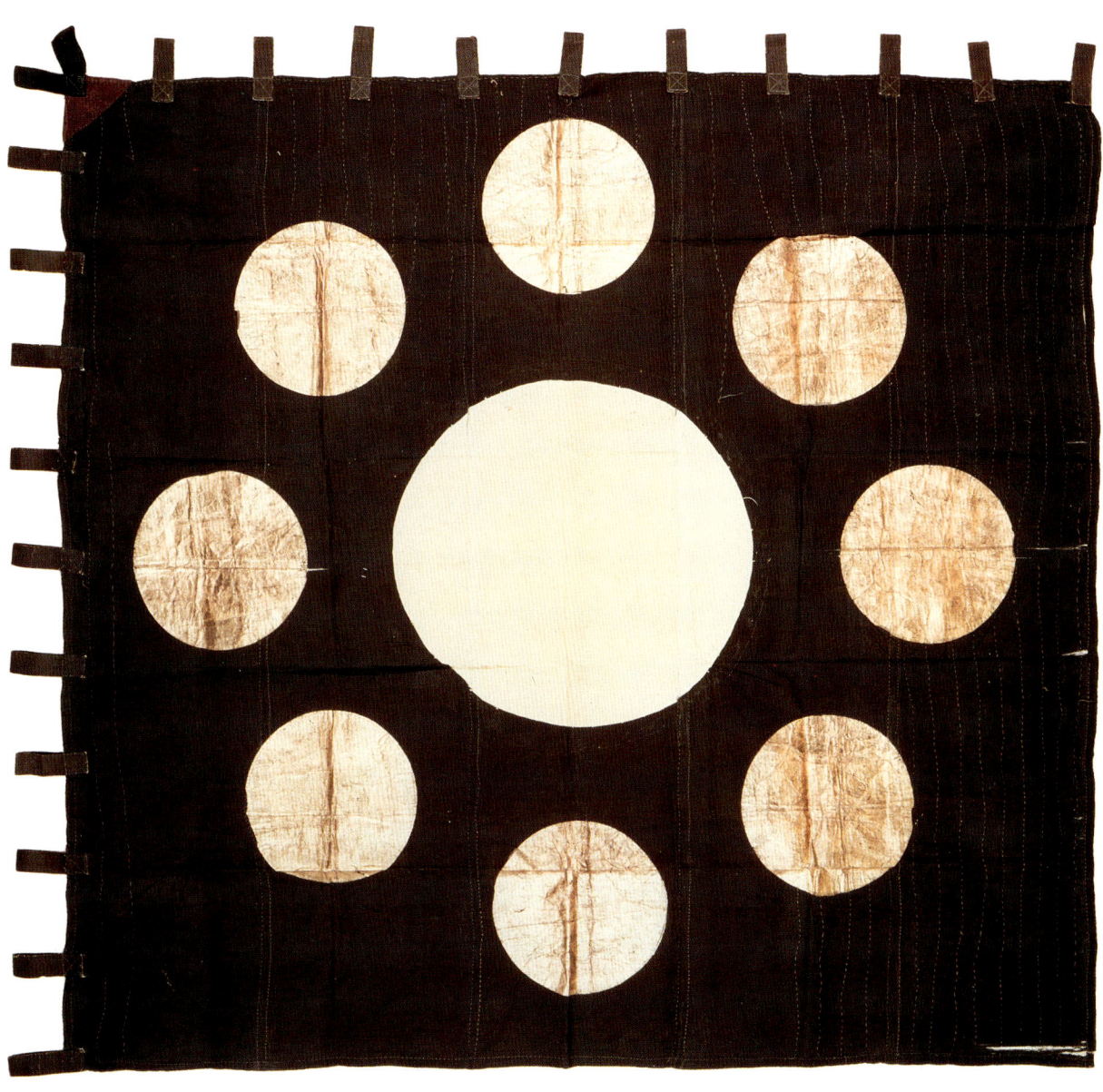

 BATTLE FLAG WITH HOSOKAWA CREST

Flags of this type were called *umajirushi*—literally, "horse markers." They were carried by foot soldiers of lower rank, attendant upon a mounted warlord, to indicate his place on the field of battle. The symbol on the flag was a matter of personal preference. Oda Nobunaga's was an umbrella; Tokugawa Ieyasu's was a gold fan—which in Japan served the function of a marshal's baton. The Hosokawas used two battle flags: the smaller one bore the Chinese character for *ari* (from Yoriari, the founder of the house); the larger one, like the flag shown here, displayed the nine-circle family crest. The fabric is silk, dyed blue; a paste resist left the circles in the original white, which were then overlaid with gold leaf. Bamboo poles passed through the straps kept the flag unfurled. Mitsunao, whose flag this was, is said to have flown it during the Shimabara Rebellion of 1638—the last battle his family was ever to fight.

Scroll Depicting Warships in Daimyo Procession (detail)

Under the Tokugawa shoguns, the heads of the great feudal baronies were required to spend every other year in Edo (Tokyo). They came and later returned to their own domains in formal procession, with their servants and retainers and bearers of baggage. The lords themselves rode or were carried in palanquins; everyone else walked. Overland to Edo from Kumamoto, the Hosokawa family seat, would have been a journey of more than a thousand miles, but early in the seventeenth century the Hosokawas began making part of that journey by ship. They built a road from Kumamoto over the mountains of central Kyūshū to the port of Tsurusaki, in Oita, on the island's east coast. The road itself, while it passed through other domains, was attached by shogunal decree to the Hosokawa fief, as a right-of-way. From Tsurusaki they sailed through the Inland Sea to Muronotsu, on the mainland, where they disembarked to take the Tōkaidō and Nakasendō highways north to the shogunal capital.

When the Hosokawas settled in Kumamoto, few, even among the daimyo, could count on a tranquil passage through the Inland Sea. It was infested with pirates. Most of the piracy, however, was controlled by a minor warlord who—like Fujitaka—had been an Ashikaga vassal. Suitable tokens of mutual respect enabled Fujitaka's heirs to sail unmolested. The domains of Kyūshū, moreover, had a long history of maritime trade with China and the Kingdom of the Ryūkyūs in Okinawa. The Hosokawas could command the services of good sailors, and of skilled shipwrights to build their growing flotilla. The shogunate allowed each daimyo a fixed number of retainers for his biennial journey; the number, of course, was a measure of the daimyo's importance. In the days of Hosokawa Yoshikuni—the last of his family to serve the obligatory year in Edo—the family fleet, depicted in this scroll, numbered fifty-seven ships.

HOSOKAWA TSUNATOSHI
1643–1714

Unidentified artist

Hanging scroll
Ink and color on silk;
inscription dated to 1715

Tsunatoshi's mother was the daughter of a *rōnin*: a samurai who had lost his master and therefore his status in the warrior class. It is not known what prompted his father, Mitsunao, to make so unpromising a connection. Tsunatoshi, in any case, was still a child when Mitsunao died, too young under shogunal law to inherit his father's fief. His chief steward, Ogasawara Tadazane, effectively governed Kumamoto until 1661.

Tsunatoshi might best be remembered for his part—albeit a minor one—in the story of "The Forty-Seven Loyal Retainers." One day in 1701, a young provincial baron named Asano, serving his term of duty at the shogun's court, attacked a courtier named Kira Yoshinaka. (Kira had demanded the usual bribes that someone in his position would expect; Asano refused, and Kira had humiliated him in public to a point where he could no longer control his rage.) Kira survived the attack, but Asano, for drawing his sword in the confines of Edo Castle, was sentenced to death; his family line was abolished and his fief confiscated. Ōishi Kuranosuke, the clan steward, and forty-seven of Asano's loyal retainers vowed revenge. On the night of December 14, 1702, they stormed Kira's villa in Edo, cut off his head, and brought it in triumph to Asano's tomb at Sengokuji, the family temple. The event captured the imagination of the Japanese, and through the centuries it has become a national epic, the last word on the subject of loyalty and sacrifice, celebrated in every medium from Kabuki to film.

The avengers were arrested. While the shogun's advisers debated what to do about them, Ōishi and seventeen of his followers were ordered to be confined in the custody of Hosokawa Tsunatoshi. Eventually they were sentenced to commit suicide, which they accepted as the reward, not the price, of their honorable vendetta. They went to that reward in the garden of Tsunatoshi's villa (with cherry blossoms, as the conventions demand, falling all around them) and were buried in the temple graveyard with their lord.

HOSOKAWA MUNETAKA
1718–1747

Unidentified artist

Hanging scroll
Ink and color on silk

Munetaka's principal claim to fame was perhaps the manner of his death: he was killed in Edo Castle, when an assassin seeking the life of another daimyo mistook Munetaka—who was wearing the same family crest—for his target.

To draw one's sword in Edo Castle was to invite the heaviest of penalties: the guilty party's entire family would forfeit its lands and titles. On the assumption that it takes two to quarrel, however, the victim's family would suffer the same fate—but only if the victim actually died on the castle grounds. It made no difference to the shogunate's curiously evenhanded sense of justice that this was a case of mistaken identity; the stroke that felled Munetaka would doom his clan as well. His vassals took their wounded lord immediately to his rooms and spent the night frantically caring for him—or at least pretending that he was still alive: there is no conclusive evidence either way. The next morning they took him in a closed palanquin to his own villa in the Nihonbashi section of the city, on the site of the present-day Bank of Japan, and did not announce his death until the following day. That legal technicality saved the Hosokawas from extinction.

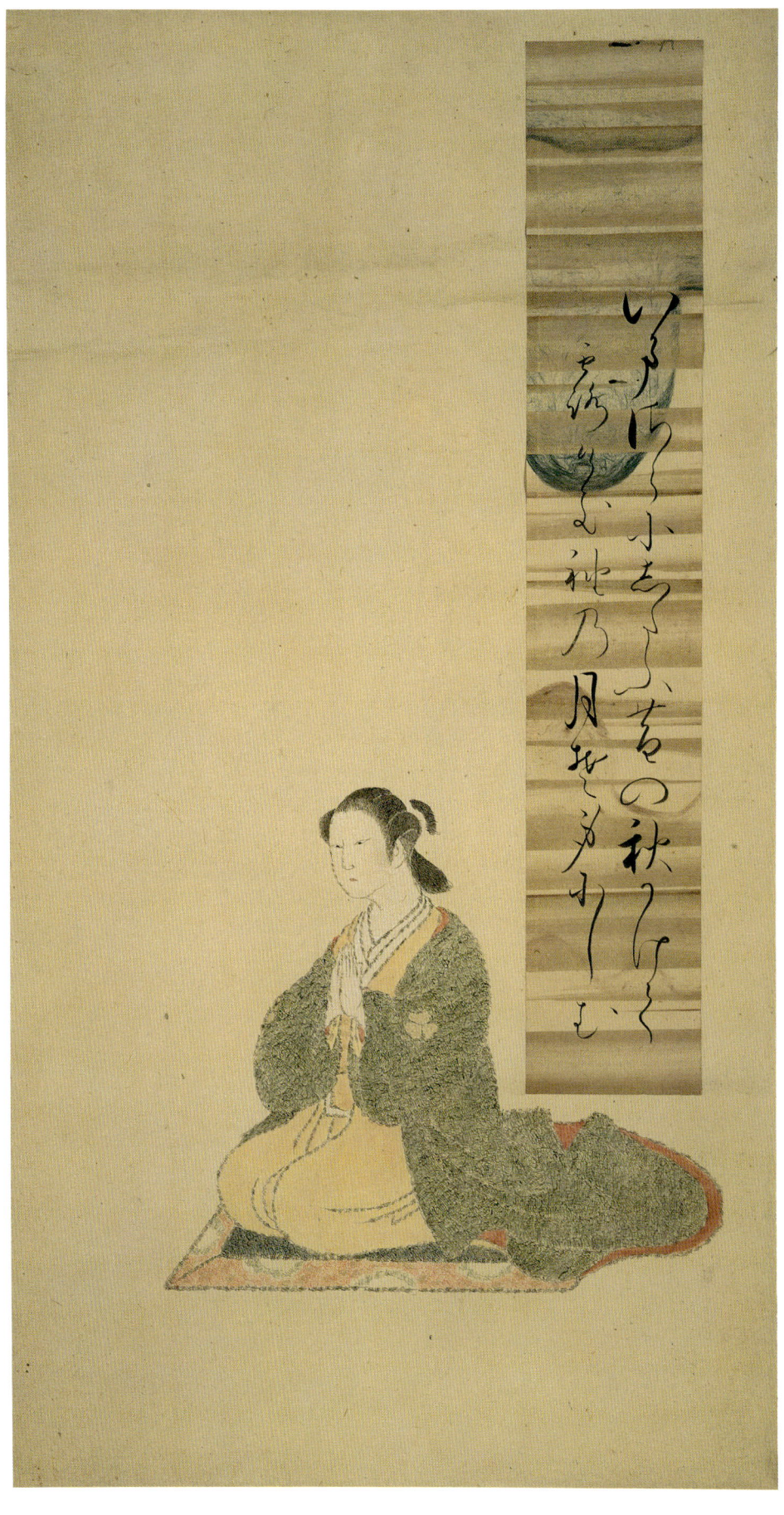

 HOSOKAWA TOMO
1720–1780

Unidentified artist

Hanging scroll
Ink and color on silk

The heads of daimyo families had their portraits painted almost as a matter of course, but it is relatively rare to have portraits of their wives. In the Hosokawa family, Fujitaka's wife, Jakō, is one exception; Tomo is another. The daughter of Tokugawa Munenao, from a branch of the shogunal family, Tomo was only twenty-seven when her husband Munetaka was assassinated. The portrait was commissioned by Shigekata, who—in the dual role of brother-in-law and adopted son—may have felt the need to pay her this special mark of consideration. Little is known of Tomo's life except what is revealed in her extensive correspondence with Shigekata. Rather than return to the family seat in Kumamoto, she chose to remain in Edo, where she died at the age of sixty.

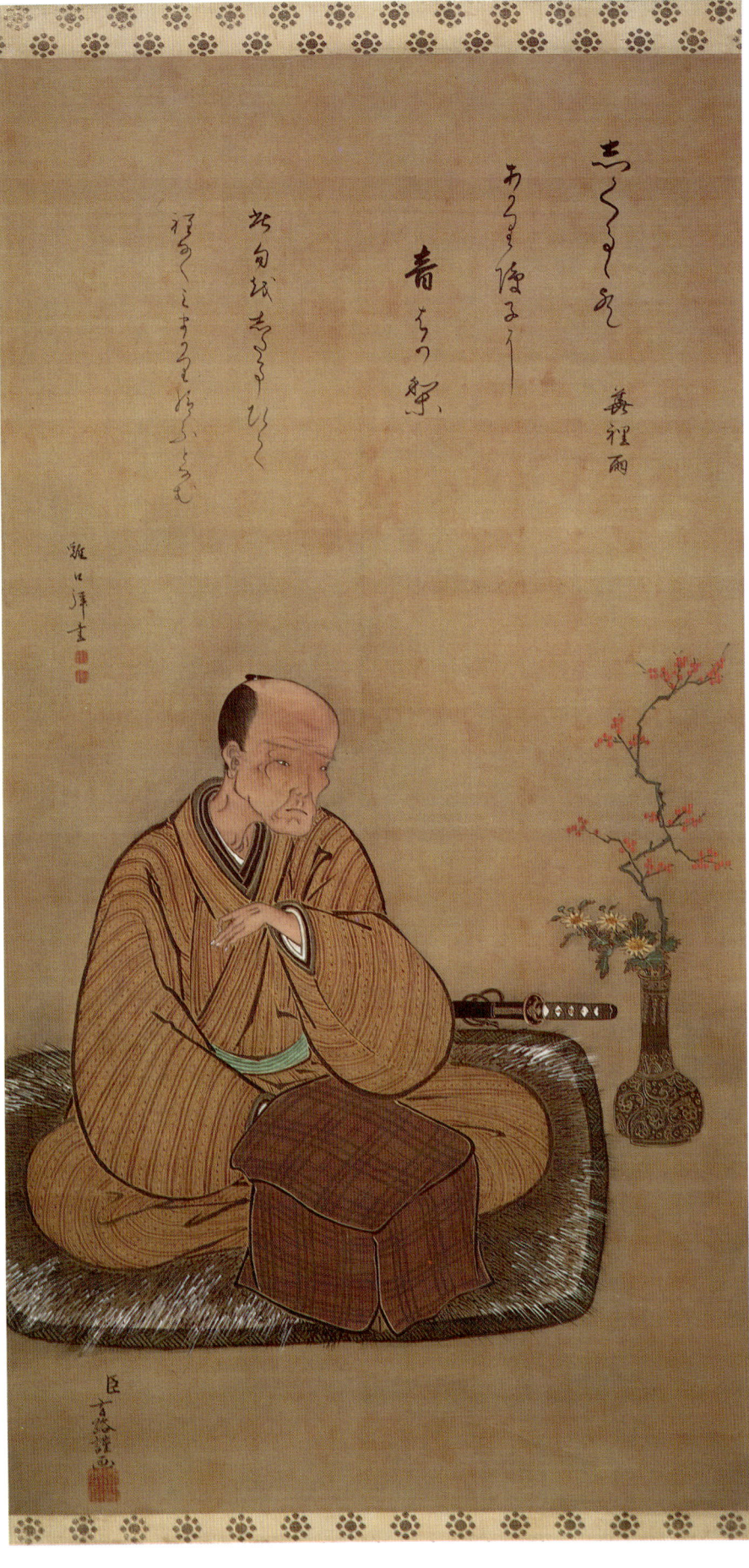

HOSOKAWA SHIGEKATA
1720–1785

Takehara Gennro

Hanging scroll
Ink and color on silk

An amateur natural scientist of extraordinary breadth and energy, Shigekata was also a visionary social reformer a century or more ahead of his time. One of his first projects as head of the family, for example, was to build hospitals in all of the major population centers of the Hosokawa fief, where anyone—farmer or samurai—could go for treatment. Elsewhere in Japan at this time, a peasant who fell ill had virtually no access to medical care of any kind. To train the necessary doctors, Shigekata founded a medical school, the ancestor of the present-day Kumamoto Medical University, and the first such school in the country. He also established an experimental herb garden in Kumamoto (which still exists), for the development of medicines that even the poor could afford. His administration of justice was equally enlightened. The feudal governments of the Tokugawa period had basically only two responses to crime—execution for murder or treason, and banishment from the fief for lesser offenses. Shigekata, however, created the nation's first modern penal system, modeled in part on Chinese civil law; long before the concept emerged in the West, his system was designed to be corrective. Penalties were codified, and convicted criminals were sent to prison for specified periods of time. In prison they were taught productive trades; the money they earned was kept and invested for them, and turned over to them on their release.

HOSOKAWA SHIGEKATA IN FORMAL COURT ATTIRE

Unidentified artist

Hanging scroll
Ink and color on silk;
inscription dated to 1786

The informal portrait of Shigekata, commissioned in the last year of his life, presents him as he probably wished to be remembered: a man who cared little for the trappings of his status, a leader of simple tastes and industrious habits. The formal portrait, painted some years earlier, is more conventional; it depicts him as he would have appeared at the imperial court in Kyoto. The mode of dress, called *ikan sokutai*, evolved in the late tenth century from an even more elaborate form of court regalia; the nobility found this simpler version more suitable for the performance of its official duties, and it was adopted for all but the highest of ceremonial occasions. Warriors and nobles wore different styles of headdress, as well as surcoats of different colors and patterns. Such distinctions also identified the wearer's rank.

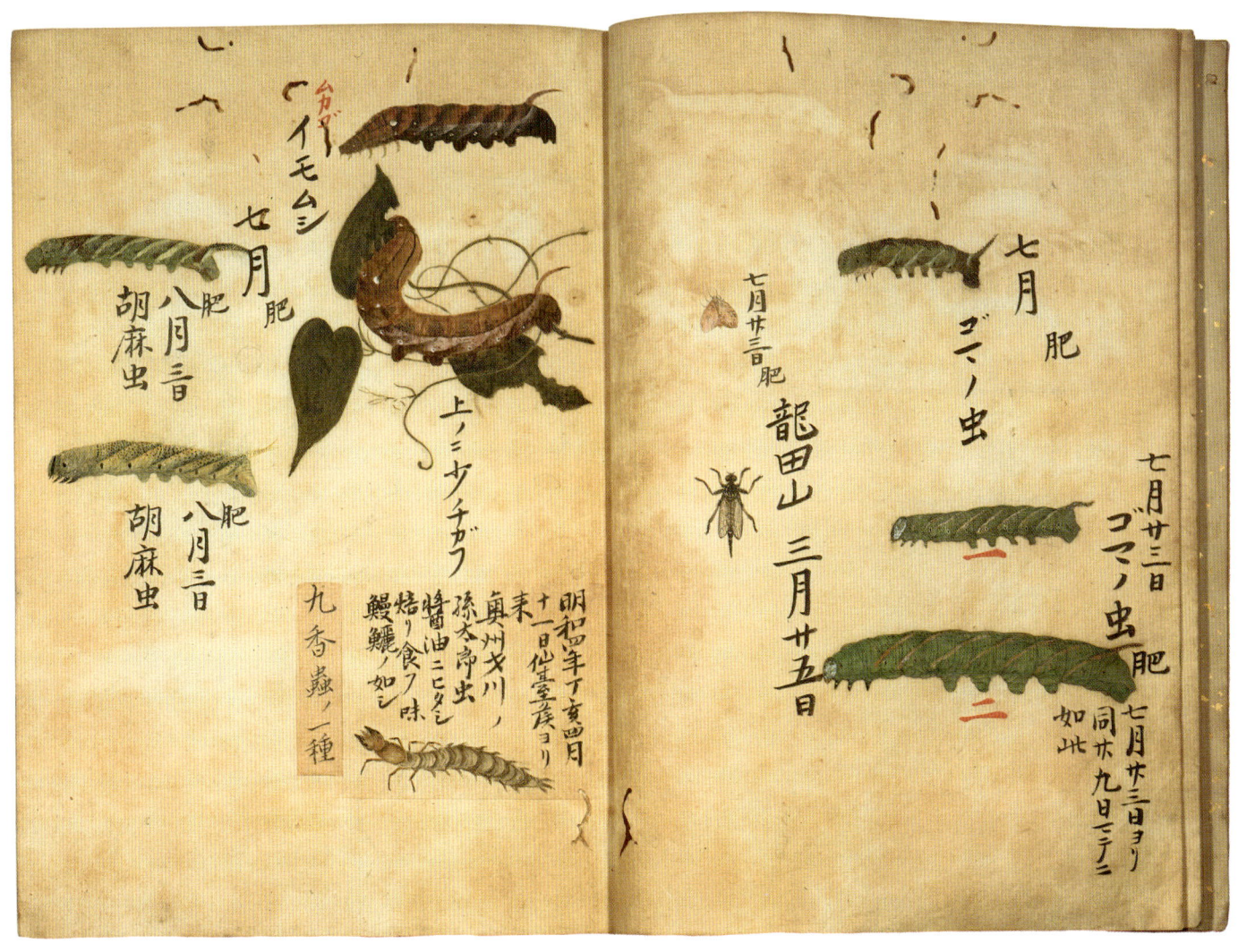

NATURE STUDIES ATTRIBUTED TO SHIGEKATA

Shigekata himself is credited with writing sixteen volumes of nature studies. Under his direction, his retainers produced some fifteen more. His interest in biology began well before he became head of the family; in his youth it was a fashionable pursuit for a young lord—much as it was in England in the nineteenth century. Their alternate years of service in the shogunal capital provided the daimyo with important opportunities to exchange the scientific information and materials they had collected, to the mutual benefit of their domains. Like some of England's titled amateur naturalists, Shigekata was far more than a hobbyist. His interests ranged over the fields of botany, zoology, and entomology. His notebooks are full of meticulous detail about when and where he acquired specimens, their dimensions and morphological changes. He drew most of the illustrations himself. Of particular interest is his drawing of the Japanese wolf, which is now extinct.

Shigekata's notebooks are in an especially fine state of preservation. They were made of paper produced in the village of Yatsushiro, on the Hosokawa domains, where two plants called *mitsumata* and *kōzo*—the latter a kind of mulberry—had been introduced from the Chinese mainland. Handmade natural-fiber papers from Yatsushiro were known all over Japan for their remarkable strength and soft, warm luster. This cottage industry (which is still practiced by a handful of households) was one of the important sources of revenue for the fief.

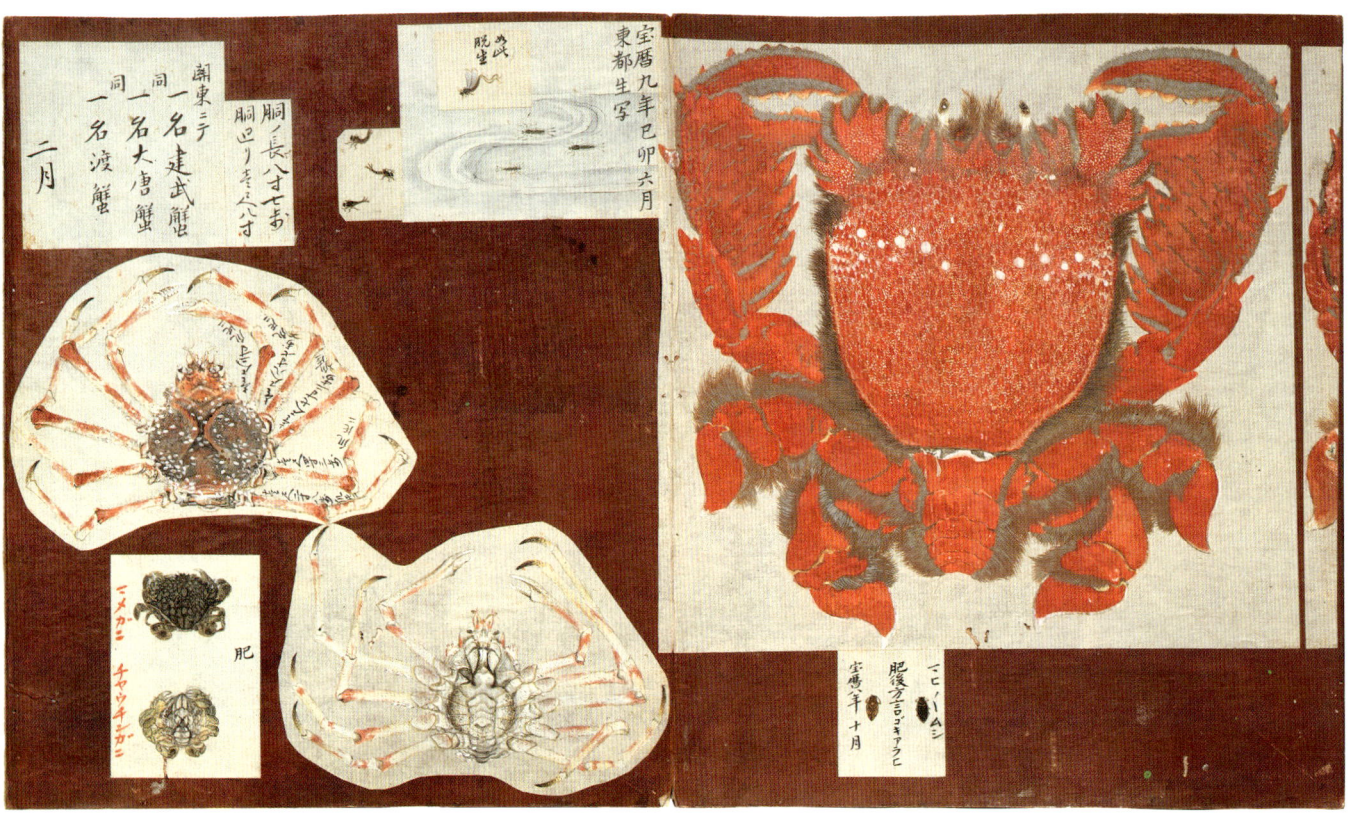

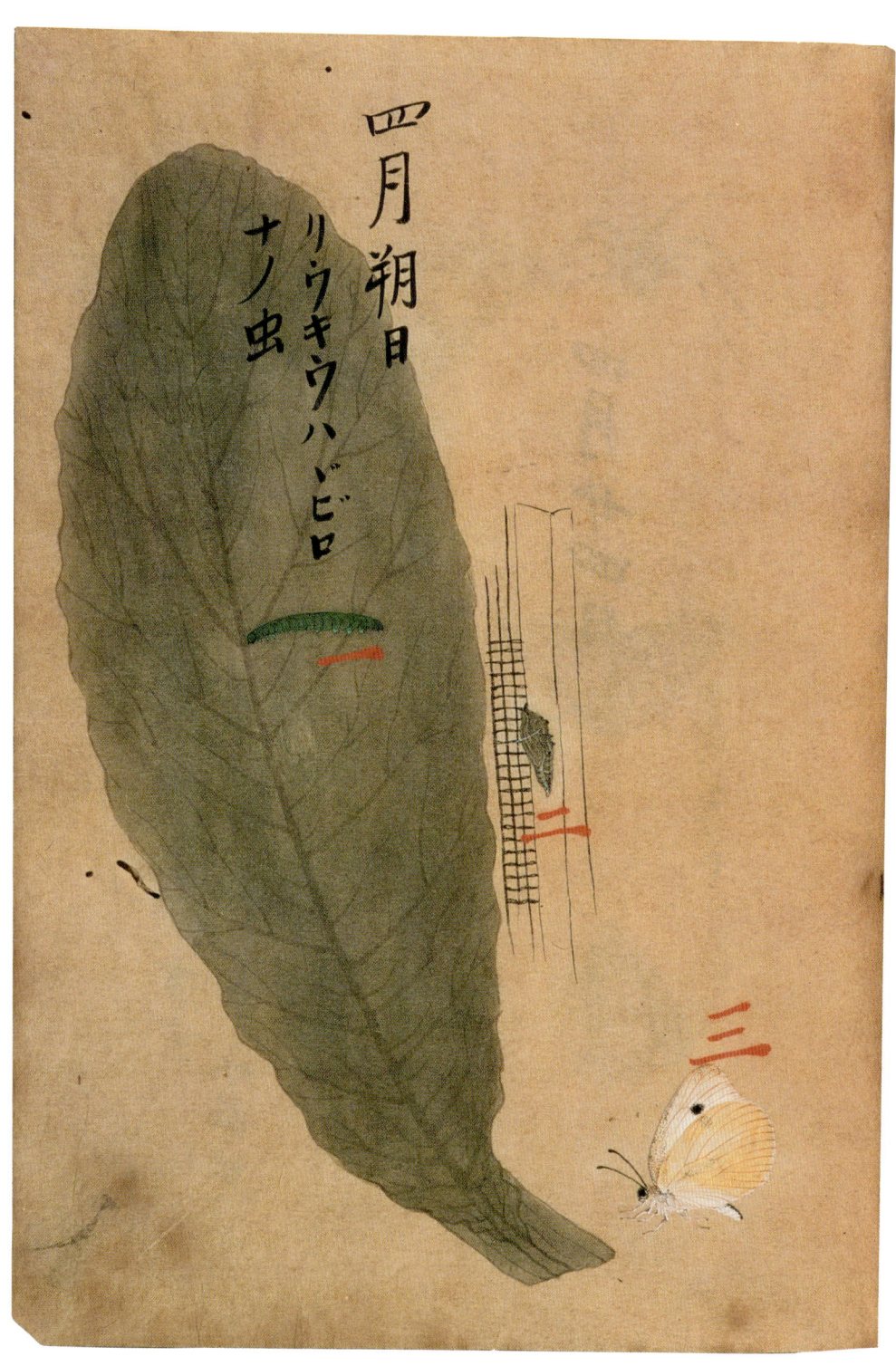

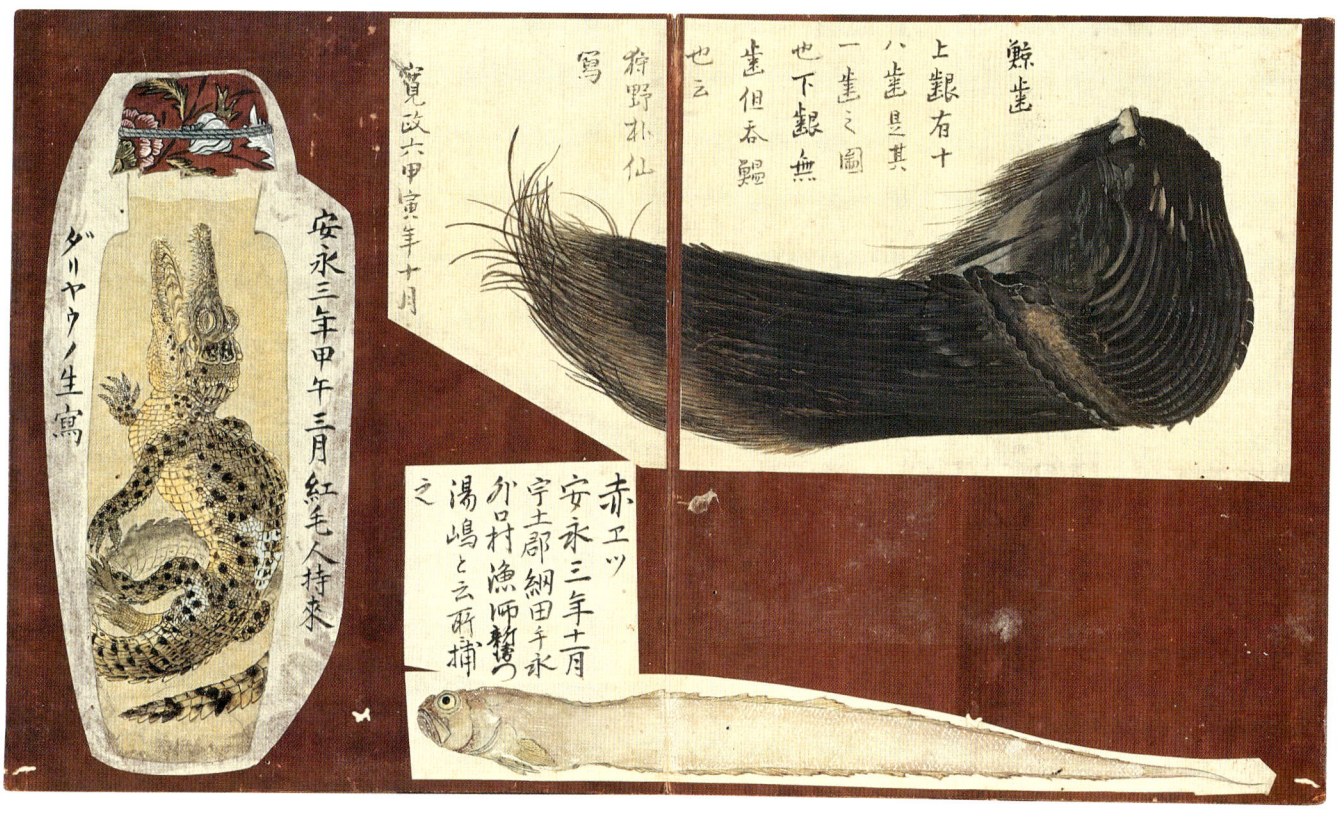

Scabbard (Saya) and Sword Mounting with Hosokawa Crest

It was the custom of every Hosokawa daimyo, as head of the clan, to commission a ceremonial scabbard like this one—modeled faithfully on the one made for Yoriari, who founded the family line. The hilt is covered in white ray-skin, with silver fittings; the sheath is lacquered wood, decorated in gold with the family crest of nine circles. Worn on solemn occasions, the scabbard was never meant to be carried into battle. This one belonged to Shigekata and appears in his formal portrait.

HOSOKAWA NARISHIGE
1759–1836

Kanou Hironobu

Hanging scroll
Ink and color on silk,
Bunsei 10 (1827)

Few heads of the Hosokawa family had less demanded of them than Narishige. He inherited, thanks to Shigekata, a wealthy and well-organized fief, and he died before the pressures on the faltering Tokugawa government plunged his country into civil war. The chief upheaval of his tenure, in fact, was natural: a long-dormant volcano near Nagasaki, in the neighboring fief, erupted and caused a tidal wave that killed some 1,500 of his people. (The mountain awoke again in November 1990, this time causing extensive property damage but very little loss of life.)

Narishige is remembered primarily as an art collector and a landscape painter. His work is interesting mainly because of its use of linear perspective—the principles of which were not yet widely known in Japan. It is not clear where Narishige acquired this approach. He may have been inspired by the woodblock printmakers, who were perhaps the first Japanese artists to experiment seriously with it. (Utagawa Toyoharu, for example, produced a series of landscapes in the 1770s that derived from his studies of German engravings.) But perspective did not really become mainstream until somewhat later: the best-known examples are Hokusai's *Thirty-Six Views of Mt. Fuji* in 1823 and Hiroshige's *Tōkaidō* series in 1834. Narishige may have been influenced more directly by the Western-style painters active in his day in Nagasaki. During the Tokugawa period, the tiny trading concession at Dejima, in Nagasaki, was Japan's only sanctioned source of things Western. Several schools of painting flourished there, from the seventeenth through the nineteenth centuries, assimilating techniques in art imported by the Dutch, and Narishige would certainly have been aware of their work.

Hosokawa Kou
1823–1826

Unidentified artist, after
Hosokawa Narishige

Hanging scroll
Ink and color on silk

This portrait of Kou, who died at the age of three in 1826, was done from a study sketched by Narishige—who was both her father and her grandfather. Narishige's child of a late second marriage, she was adopted by Naritatsu, Narishige's oldest son, who doted on Kou and was devastated by her death. Narishige commissioned a number of similar memorial portraits, which were sent to the various temples under Hosokawa patronage—the Kōmyōji in Kamakura, the Taishōji in Kumamoto, the Tōkaiji in Tokyo—to comfort Naritatsu whenever he visited one of them to worship.

MATSUDAIRA TAI
1793–1824

Unidentified artist

Hanging scroll
Ink and color on silk

Naritatsu's oldest daughter, Tai, was born not to his official wife but to his concubine, Yamashina. A member of the nobility, Yamashina was Naritatsu's consort during the period of his compulsory residence in the shogunal capital at Edo. Tai was married to Matsudaira Naritsune, lord of the fief of Dewa, in the far northeastern part of the country. The marriage ended in divorce, and Tai returned to Kumamoto. This was an obvious embarrassment; the failure of an arranged match between two important daimyo houses was bound to have political repercussions, but there are no records to indicate what happened or why. As soon as it could be arranged, Naritatsu remarried Tai to the courtier Ichijo Tadayoshi, chief adviser to the Emperor and a close associate. (The Hosokawa connections with the nobility were, as they had been for centuries, especially strong.) Tai died in Kyoto at the age of thirty-one.

HOSOKAWA YOSHIKUNI
1835–1876

Goseda Yoshimatu

Hanging scroll
Ink and color on paper,
1879

The Meiji Restoration took its toll of Yoshikuni. Never robust, he exhausted what little strength he had in the vain effort to mediate between the rival court and shogunal factions. The open warfare he had hoped to avert was inevitable. At best, Yoshikuni could only keep his own family off the battlefield when the court faction and its coalition of clans from western Japan overthrew the shogunate. One of the first concerns of the new Meiji government was to dismantle the system of feudal domains. The Hosokawa fief became the province of Kumamoto, and Yoshikuni was appointed its first governor. In failing health, he resigned that office in 1870, retiring as head of the family at the same time and passing both roles to his younger brother Morihisa.

Yoshikuni spent the last years of his life in Tokyo, where the Meiji government had required him to make his official residence. With the abolition of the fief, the Hosokawas surrendered Kumamoto Castle to the imperial army—only to see it destroyed, the year after Yoshikuni died, in the Satsuma Rebellion.

Saigō Takamori, born in the fief of Satsuma, had been one of the key figures in the coalition that overthrew the Tokugawa shogunate. Commanding general of the imperial army, and briefly acting head of state, he had resigned in 1873 in a dispute over the government's policy on relations with Korea and returned to Kyūshū with several thousand loyal followers from his former clan. Fearing what seemed to be an attempt to build a private army, the other Meiji leaders turned against Saigō. That conflict blossomed into open rebellion, which came to a head when Saigō led a force of some 30,000 against the small imperial garrison at Kumamoto. The garrison's 4,000-odd defenders held out for fifty days, until government reinforcements arrived to crush the revolt. In the meantime, the garrison had burned its stores and munitions to keep them from the rebels, and artillery fire had largely destroyed what was left of the castle. Hosokawa daimyos had ruled from this seat for almost four hundred years, and now it was gone.

After World War II, the government of Kumamoto rebuilt the castle, in concrete, and on a far smaller scale. History finds curious ways of repeating itself: Kumamoto evolved from a province to a prefecture; a century later, in 1983, Hosokawa Morihiro, the oldest son of the present head of the family, was elected its governor. He resigned toward the end of his second term, early in 1991, to chair a subcommittee of the government's Provisional Council for the Promotion of Administrative Reform.

For Further Reading

Akamatsu, Paul. *Meiji 1868: Revolution and Counter-Revolution in Japan.* Translated by Miriam Kochan. London: George Allen & Unwin, Ltd., 1972.

Anderson, L. J. *Japanese Armour.* London: The Arms and Armour Press, 1968.

Beasley, W. G. *The Modern History of Japan.* London: Weidenfeld & Nicolson, 1973.

Berry, Mary Elizabeth. *Hideyoshi.* Cambridge, Mass.: Harvard University Press, 1982.

Bolitho, Harold. *Treasures Among Men: The Feudal Daimyo in Tokugawa Japan.* New Haven, Conn.: Yale University Press, 1974.

Elison, George, and Bardwell L. Smith, eds. *Warlords, Artists, and Commoners: Japan in the Sixteenth Century.* Honolulu: University of Hawaii Press, 1981.

Hall, John Whitney. *Japan from Prehistory to Modern Times.* New York: Delacorte Press, 1970.

Hall, John Whitney, and Takeishi Toyoda, eds. *Japan in the Muromachi Age.* Berkeley: University of California Press, 1977.

Komparu, Kunio. *The Noh Theater: Principles and Perspectives.* Translated by Jane Corddry. New York: Weatherhill, 1983.

Mass, Jeffrey P., and William B. Hauser, eds. *The Bakufu in Japanese History.* Stanford, Calif.: Stanford University Press, 1985.

Minnich, Helen Benton, and Shojiro Nomura. *Japanese Costume and the Makers of Its Elegant Tradition.* Rutland, Vt.: Charles E. Tuttle Co., 1963.

Shimizu, Yoshiaki, ed. *Japan: The Shaping of Daimyo Culture, 1185–1868.* Washington, D.C.: National Gallery of Art, 1988.

Stanley-Baker, Joan. *Japanese Art.* London: Thames and Hudson, 1984.

Varly, H. Paul. *The Ōnin War.* New York: Columbia University Press, 1967.

Yamamura, Kozo, ed. *The Cambridge History of Japan.* Volume 3: *Medieval Japan.* Cambridge: Cambridge University Press, 1990.

Index

Italicized page numbers refer to illustrations.

Akamatsu Mitsusuke, 20
Akechi Mitsuhide, 23, 24
Amakusa Shiro, 27
Asano Naganori, 81
Ashikaga Takauji, 15, 16–17, 19, 49
Ashikaga Yoshiaki, 23
Ashikaga Yoshiakira, 19
Ashikaga Yoshiharu, 22
Ashikaga Yoshikatsu, 20
Ashikaga Yoshimasa, 20, 21
Ashikaga Yoshimitsu, 19, 20, 43, 45
Ashikaga Yoshinori, 20
Ashikaga Yoshiteru, 23
Ashikaga shogunate, 15, 17, 19, 23, 39, 55, 79

Chōjirō I, 59

Edo Castle, 81, 83
Eisei-Bunko, 10, 12, 13, 32, 34, 65

Fillmore, Millard, 29
Fujiwara family, 33

Go-Daigo, Emperor, 15–16, 17
Go-Komatsu, Emperor, 20, 41
Goseda Yoshimatu, 107
Gracia. *See* Hosokawa Tama (Gracia)

Hara Castle, 27
Hatakeyama Mochikuni, 21
Hatakeyama family, 19
Hirohito, Emperor, 33
Hishida Shunsō, 32
Hitotsubashi Yoshinobu, 31
Hōjō family, 15, 16
Hosokawa Fujitaka (Yūsai), 18, 22–23, 24, 26, 31, *50*, 51, 53, 55, 67, 79, 85
Hosokawa Harutoshi, 18, 28
Hosokawa Jakō, *54*, 55, 85

Hosokawa Katsumoto, 18, 20–21
Hosokawa Kou, *102*, 103
Hosokawa Masaari, 18
Hosokawa Masamoto, 18, 49
Hosokawa Mitsumoto, 18
Hosokawa Mitsunao, 18, 28, 77, 81
Hosokawa Mochiari, 18
Hosokawa Mochiyuki, 18, 20
Hosokawa Morihiro, 107
Hosokawa Morihisa, 18, 107
Hosokawa Morisada, 9, 11, 13, 18, 32–34, 65
Hosokawa Morishige, 18
Hosokawa Moritatsu, 18, 32
Hosokawa Motoari, 18
Hosokawa Mototsune, 18, 22
Hosokawa Munetaka, 18, 28, *82*, 83, 85
Hosokawa Narimori, 18
Hosokawa Narishige, 18, 28–29, *100*, 101, 103
Hosokawa Naritatsu, 18, 29, 103, 105
Hosokawa Nobunori, 18, 28
Hosokawa Noriharu, 18
Hosokawa Shigekata, 12, 13, 18, 28, 85, *86*, 87, 88, 89, 91, 99, 101
Hosokawa Sumimoto, 12, 18, *48*, 49
Hosokawa Tadaoki (Sansai), 13, 18, 23–24, 25, 26–27, 53, 56, 57, 59, 61, 63, 65, 67, 69, 71
Hosokawa Tadatoshi, 18, 26–27, 28, 29, 70, 71, 75
Hosokawa Tama (Gracia), 23, 24, 25, 27, 63, 65
Hosokawa Tomo, *84*, 85
Hosokawa Tsunatoshi, 18, 28, *80*, 81
Hosokawa Tsuneari, 18
Hosokawa Yoriari, 17, 18, 20, 22, *38*, 39, 41, 77, 99
Hosokawa Yoriharu, 16, 17, 18
Hosokawa Yorimoto, 18
Hosokawa Yorinaga, 18

Hosokawa Yoriyuki, 17, 18, 19–20, 39, 42, 43, 47, 49
Hosokawa Yoshikuni, 12, 18, 29, 30–31, 32, 33, 79, *106*, 107

Ichijo Tadayoshi, 105
Ishida Mitsunari, 25
Ishida family, 25, 69

Kabuki, 10, 81
Kagura-ga-oka, Battle of, 22
Kanou Hironobu, 101
Kato family, 71
Kira Yoshinaka, 81
Kiyomasa Kato, 27
Kōmei, Emperor, 30, 31
Konoe Fumimaro, Prince, 33
Kumamoto Castle, *27*, 32, 107

Matsudaira Naritsune, 105
Matsudaira Tai, *104*, 105
Meiji Restoration, 22, 29, 31, 107
Mitsubuchi Harukazu, 22
Miyamoto Mushshi, 27–28
Mori family, 30
Murasaki Shikibu, 22
Muromachi period, 17, 19, 20, 22, 49, 53
Myōchin family, 53

Nimanzan, Battle of, 20
Nitta Yoshisada, 16
Noh theater, 10, 13, 19, 45, 47
Numata Mitsukane, 55

Oda Nobunaga, 23, 24, 25, 59, 77
Ogasawara Tadazane, 81
Ogasawara family, 27
Ōishi Kuranosuke, 81
Ōnin War, 21

Perry, Matthew, 29, *30*

Saigō Takamori, 107
Sansai. *See* Hosokawa Tadaoki (Sansai)
Satsuma Rebellion, 107
Sekigahara, Battle of, 25–26, 30, 67, 68, 69
Sen no Rikyū, 25, 57, 59
Sen Sotan, 59
Shiba family, 19
Shimabara Rebellion, 26–27, 77
Shimazu family, 30–31, 69
Shimomura Kanzen, 32

Takamatsu-no-miya, Prince, 33
Takayama Ukon, 25
Takehara Gennro, 87
Tanabe Castle, 24, 51, 55
Tashiro Tōho, 51
Tea ceremony, 13, 19, 25, 30–31, 57, 59
Tojo Hideki, 33
Tokugawa Iemitsu, 71
Tokugawa Iemochi, 31
Tokugawa Ieyasu, 24, 25–26, 30, 69, 71, 77
Tokugawa Munenao, 85
Tokugawa shogunate, 17, 22, 25, 26, 28, 29, 30, 31, 71, 79, 87, 101, 107
Toyotomi Hideyoshi, 24, 25, 26, 57, 59, 69
Toyotomi family, 26

Uesugi family, 25, 69

Yamashina, 105
Yokohama Taikan, 32
Yūsai. *See* Hosokawa Fujitaka (Yūsai)

Edited by Frances K. Stevenson and Dru Dowdy

Designed by the Watermark Design Office, Alexandria, Virginia, and electronically typeset in Berkeley Old Style Book and Medium

Printed on eighty-pound Centura Dull paper by Collins Lithographing and Printing Company, Baltimore, Maryland